J. CREE FISCHER

PIANO TUNING

A SIMPLE AND ACCURATE METHOD
FOR AMATEURS

DOVER PUBLICATIONS, INC.
NEW YORK

Published in Canada by General Publishing
Company, Ltd., 30 Lesmill Road, Don Mills,
Toronto, Ontario.
Published in the United Kingdom by Constable
and Company, Ltd., 10 Orange Street, London
WC 2.

This Dover edition, first published in 1975, is
a republication of the work originally published
in Philadelphia in 1907. The following sections
have been omitted from the present edition because they were out-of-date: Practical Application
of Piano Tuning as a Profession, Business Hints,
Ideas in Advertising, and Charges for Services.
This edition is reprinted by special arrangement
with Theodore Presser Company, Presser Place,
Bryn Mawr, Pennsylvania, publisher of the original
edition.

International Standard Book Number: 0-486-23267-0
Library of Congress Catalog Card Number: 75-14759

Manufactured in the United States of America
Dover Publications, Inc.
180 Varick Street
New York, N. Y. 10014

PREFACE.

For some years past a lack of competent men in the profession of Piano Tuning has been generally acknowledged. This may be accounted for as follows: The immense popularity of the piano and the assiduous efforts of factories and salesmen have led to the result that nearly every well-to-do household is furnished with an instrument. To supply this demand the annual production and sale for the year 1906 is estimated at three hundred thousand pianos in the United States. These pianos must be tuned many times in the factory before they are shipped to the salesroom; there they must be kept in tune until sold. When, finally, they take up their permanent abode in the homes of the purchasers, they should be given the attention of the tuner at least twice a year. This means work for the tuner. But this is not all. Presuming that the average life of the piano is about fifty years, it is evident that there exists in this country an accumulation of instruments variously estimated at from four to five millions. This means *more work for tuners*.

While production and accumulation have been increasing, there has been little, if any, effort made to provide tuners to look after the needs of this ever-increasing number of instruments, no provision for the thorough instruction of the learner of Piano Tuning, outside the walls of the factories, and of the few musical colleges where the art is taught. Doubtless there are many persons who are by nature well adapted to this agreeable and profitable occupation—persons who would make earnest effort to acquire the necessary skill and its honest application if they had a favorable opportunity. Musical colleges in which tuning is taught are few and far between; piano factories are built for the purpose of producing pianos and not tuners, for mechanics and laborers and not for teachers and pupils; furthermore, very little fine tuning is done in the factory; rough tuning is the bulk of the work there, and a long apprenticeship in the factory, with its meager advantages, is rarely sufficient to meet the demands of the would-be-thorough tuner. This may account, in part, for the fact that many who are incompetent are following this profession, and that there is an increasing demand for tuners of skill.

In view of these facts the author came to the opinion that if a course of instruction were prepared which would demonstrate clearly the many abstruse details of the art in an interesting and comprehensible way, it would be appreciated by those who are desirous to learn. Acting upon this impulse, he began the preparation of such a course.

The present book is the outgrowth of a course of instruction, used successfully with pupils from various parts of the United States and Canada, conducted partly by correspondence, partly at the school directed by the author. Although it has been necessary to revise the course somewhat for publication in the present form, no essential matter has been omitted and much has been added.

In preparing this course of study the utmost effort has been made to present the various topics in the clearest, most comprehensive manner, literary excellence being a secondary consideration.

While the book is designed for self-instruction, the systematic arrangement of the text, and the review questions with each lesson, suggest its use as a text-book for schools and colleges which give personal training in the care of the piano.

To the talented individual of either sex who is ambitious to acquire a dignified and profitable profession, to the scientifically-inclined musician who is eager to learn the fundamental principles underlying all musical harmony, and finally to the non-professional who loves to read because of a fondness for science, the book is submitted; if it should prove a boon to the former, a benefit to the second, or a pleasure to the latter, I shall feel rewarded for the work of its preparation.

THE AUTHOR.

CONTENTS.

LESSON I.

INTRODUCTION.

Undoubtedly every human being is fitted for some sphere of usefulness—some industry by which he can benefit mankind and support himself in comfort. Just what we are fitted for must, almost invariably, be decided by ourselves; and the sooner the better, else we may plod among the thousands whose lives are miserable failures for the reason that "they have missed their calling."

In the consideration of Piano Tuning as a profession, one should first determine if he possesses the necessary qualifications, the most important of which are a musical ear and some degree of mechanical ability. Having these, all else may be acquired by study. It is not necessary to possess a musical education or to be a musician; although a knowledge of music will be found a great aid. Still, an elementary knowledge of the principles of music is a necessity to the student of this course, as it has been found impossible to avoid the use of a few technical terms. In most cases, however, they are set forth in such a way that they will be readily apprehended by anyone who has even a slight knowledge of the fundamental principles of music.

In teaching Piano Tuning, it is the custom of the "Central School of Piano Tuning," for which these lessons were originally prepared, to have all students prepare two lessons in harmony as a test of their acquaintance with the intervals and chords used in tuning. The lessons are not difficult, and they embody only those principles which are essential to the proper understanding of the key-board: the intervals of the diatonic scale and the major common chord in the twelve different keys, C, D, E, F, G, A, B, B-flat, D-flat, E-flat, G-flat, and A-flat. In connection with the harmony lessons, we use as a text-book "Clarke's Harmony,"* and the student is required to master the first two chapters and prepare manuscripts upon each of the lessons. Below is a number

---

* Published by Theodore Presser, Philadelphia, Pa.

of the most important questions selected from those lessons upon which manuscripts have been written:

1. Every white key on the piano represents an "absolute pitch." By what names are these pitches known? How are the black keys named?

2. How many tones constitute the diatonic scale? Give numerical names.

3. Intervals are measured by steps and half-steps. How many steps from 1 to 3 in the diatonic scale? 1 to 4? 1 to 5? 3 to 5? 5 to 8? 1 to 8?

4. Why is there no black key between E and F, and between B and C?

5. From 1 to 3 is called an interval of a third; from 3 to 5, also a third; from 1 to 5, a fifth: they are so called because they include, respectively, three and five members of the diatonic scale. What is the interval 3 to 6? 2 to 5? 5 to 8? 2 to 6? 1 to 8?

6. Thirds are of two kinds: major (larger) thirds embrace two whole-steps; minor (smaller) thirds embrace a step and a half. What kind of a third is 1–3 in the diatonic scale? 2—4? 3—5? 6—8?

7. What do we mean by the term, Fundamental of a chord? What is added to it to complete the common chord?

8. What absolute pitches comprise the common chord of C? What kind of interval between the first two members? What between the first and last? What between the second and last?

9. What tones would you use if told to strike the common chord of C in four-part, close harmony, using the fundamental for the highest tone?

10. How many keys (white and black) are there be-

tween the fundamental and the third? How many between the third and the fifth? How many between the fundamental and the fifth when the fifth is played above the fundamental?

11. How many keys (white and black) are there between two keys comprising a perfect fourth?

12. (Most important of all.) What keys of the piano keyboard comprise the common chord founded upon G as the fundamental? Upon F? Upon F#? Upon G#? Upon B♭? Upon D♭? Upon E♭? Upon D? Upon E? Upon A? Upon B?

If one is able to answer these questions correctly he is qualified to begin the study of Piano Tuning.

LESSON II.

GENERAL CONSTRUCTION OF THE PIANO; SOMETHING OF ITS EVOLUTION AND HISTORY.

The piano of today is, unquestionably, the most perfect, and consequently the most popular and beloved of all musical instruments.

> That enchanting Queen of the home,
>   Whose place in the hearts of the family
> Is as dear as though it could speak
>   In words of joy and sorrow,
> Sadness or consolation;
>   Soothing, animating, enrapturing,
> Charming away the soul
>   From its worldly weight of cares,
> And wafting it softly
>   Into the realm of celestial dreams.

The untiring efforts of genius for over a century have succeeded in producing a musical instrument that falls little short of perfection. Yet other inventions and improvements are sure to come, for we are never content with "good enough."

The student of these lessons may, in his practice, discover defective mechanical action and by his ingenuity be able to improve it; he may likewise see where an improvement can be made in acoustic construction; where a better scale can be drawn; or where different and perhaps new materials may be used for the component parts of the instrument. The possibilities are numerous along these lines, and in addition to bestowing a favor upon the general public, the man who has the originality to produce something new, places himself beyond want.

The inevitable inference is that the piano is an evolution of the harp principle. This instrument was known centuries previous to the Christian era. From the best history obtainable, we learn that about three hundred years ago, the first effort was made to interpose a mechanical contrivance between the performer and the strings whereby it would only be necessary to strike the keys to produce tone from the strings, thereby decreasing the difficulty in finding the strings and picking them with the fingers, and greatly increasing the possibilities in musical rendition.

History gives credit to Italy for the first productions of this kind, about 1600 A. D., when the faculty of music was beginning to manifest itself more boldly. Scientists saw that wonderful developments were possible, and we have reason to believe that experiments were made in England, France, Germany and all civilized countries about this time, for the production of the instrument which we call, in this day, a Pianoforte. (*Piano e forte:* soft and loud.)

At this time communication between the different countries was, of course, slow and uncertain, and experiments of this kind were probably unknown outside of the immediate neighborhood in which they were tried; therefore, much valuable and interesting history has not come to light. However, from the specimens which we have had the pleasure of seeing, and some of which we have had the opportunity to work on, we infer that about the same line of difficulties presented themselves to all of these early experimenters, most of which were not efficiently overcome until in the last century, and the most important of which it fell to the lot of American inventors to overcome.

Some of these early instruments were not even provided with dampers for stopping the tone when the key was released; consequently, when a number of keys were struck in succession, the tone continued from all, so long as the strings would vibrate. The strings and sound-board being very light, the sustaining qualities were meager compared to those of the modern piano; consequently the dampers were not so much missed as they would be if removed from a modern upright or grand, which would surely render them unfit for use.

In the first attempts at piano building, the difficulties to be overcome may be enumerated as follows: The frames were not strong enough to resist the tension of the strings; they were made almost entirely of wood which yields to the pull of the strings and is subject to climatic changes; the scale was very imperfect, that is, the length, tension and weight of the strings were not properly proportioned, the result being a different quality of tone from different portions of the keyboard; the actions were either heavy and imperfect, or too light to produce sufficient vibration; the proper point upon the strings for the hammers to strike and for the dampers to bear had not yet been ascertained; the preparation and seasoning of the wood for the different parts of the instrument had not received sufficient attention.

One cannot conceive how difficult it is to produce something that has never existed, until he tries. The requirements necessary to such results as are obtainable from the modern piano are numerous and rigid and the result of many costly experiments.

Probably the most important essential in piano building is the production of a frame of such strength and stability that the enormous tension of the strings is completely resisted in all parts of the scale. In many of the cheaper pianos of this day, the lack of this essential manifests itself in an annoying degree to the piano tuner. In tuning, the workman "brings up" his temperament in the middle of the instrument; in most cases the temperament stands all right. He next tunes the treble, then the bass; after doing his work perfectly he will often find that the treble fell somewhat while he was bringing up the bass; or, in a few cases, he may find that the treble sharpened, thus showing that there was yielding of the frame. Of course, this defect might be overcome by using an extremely heavy metal plate and wooden frame; but the commercial side of the question, in this day, calls for lightness in the instrument as a check to the expense of production, and, consequently, pianos that are "made to sell" are often much too light to fulfil this requirement.

In the upright piano, the back frame of wood is first made; at the top of this is the pin-block, sometimes called the wrest-plank. This is composed of several layers of wood firmly glued together with the grain running in different directions to prevent splitting and warping. Into this plank the tuning pins are driven. The sound-board is fitted firmly into this frame of wood below the pin-block.

Next, the strong metal plate is secured to the frame by large bolts and screws. Openings are left in the plate for the bridges, which project from the sound-board beyond the metal plate; also for the tuning pins, action bracket bolts, etc.

At the lower end of the plate, and just below the bridges,* the hitchpins are driven firmly into holes drilled to receive them. Their purpose is to support the lower ends of the strings. The bass strings are separate, and each has a loop with which to fasten it to the hitchpin. In the treble, one piece of wire forms two strings; the two ends are secured to the

---

* There are two sections of the lower bridge, one for the treble and one for the overstrung bass.

tuning pins above, and the string is simply brought around the hitchpin. The bridges communicating with the sound-board are at the lower end of the sound-board. Notice, there is a portion of the length of each string between the bridge and the hitchpin.

At the upper end of the strings, a "bearing-bar," situated between the tuning pins and upper bridge, is attached to the pin-block by screws which draw it inward; its function is to hold the strings firmly in position. You will notice that the lengths of the strings, above the bearing-bar, vary considerably, even in the three strings comprising the unison. (We will speak of the effect of this in tuning, farther on.)

After that portion of the case is completed which forms the key-bed or action frame, we are ready to set in the

ACTION.

By this is meant the keys and all those intricate parts which convey the motion of the key to the hammers which strike the strings, and the dampers which mute them.

The requisites of the action are as follows:

The keys must descend quickly and easily at the touch of the performer, giving quick response.

The weight of the hammer must be properly proportioned to the strings it causes to vibrate.

The hammer must rebound after striking the string. (Where the hammer remains against the string, thereby preventing vibration, the term "blocking" is used to designate the fault.)

The action must be capable of quick repetition; that is, when a key is struck a number of times in quick succession, it must respond perfectly every time.

After striking and rebounding from the string, the hammer should not fall to its lowest position where it rests when not in use, as this would prevent quick repetition. For catching the hammer at a short distance from the string, a felted piece of wood suspended on a wire, called the back check, rises when the key is depressed, and returns when the key is released, allowing the hammer to regain its resting position.

A damper, for stopping the tone of the string when a key is released, must leave the string just before the hammer strikes, and return the instant the key is released.

A means must be provided for releasing all the dampers from the strings at the will of the performer.

The loud pedal, as it is called, but more properly, the damper pedal, accomplishes this end by raising the dampers from the strings.

In the square and the grand piano, the action is under the sound-board, while the strings are over it; so the hammers are made to strike through an opening in the sound-board. In the upright, the strings are between the action and the sound-board; so no opening is necessary in the latter.

The "trap-action" consists of the pedals and the parts which convey motion to the action proper.

QUESTIONS ON LESSON II.

1. What have been some of the salient obstacles necessary to overcome in producing the perfected piano?
2. Of what use are the dampers? Explain their mechanical action.
3. Mention several of the qualities necessary to a good action.
4. Describe the building of an upright piano.
5. Contrast the musical capacity and peculiar characteristics of the piano with those of the organ, which has the same keyboard.

LESSON III.

TECHNICAL NAMES AND USES OF THE PARTS OF THE UPRIGHT PIANO ACTION.

In the practice of piano tuning, the first thing is to ascertain if the action is in first-class condition. The tuner must be able to detect, locate and correct the slightest defect in any portion of the instrument. Any regulating or repairing of the action should be attended to before tuning the instrument; the latter should be the final operation. As a thorough knowledge of regulating and repairing is practically indispensable to the professional tuner, the author has spared neither means, labor nor research to make this part of the lessons very complete, and feels sure that it will meet with the hearty approval of most, if not all, students. The piano tuner who knows nothing of regulating and repairing will miss many an opportunity to earn extra money.

The illustration accompanying this lesson is from a Wessell, Nickel and Gross Upright action. This

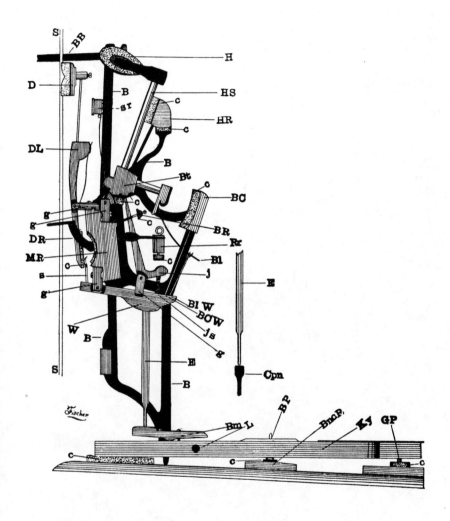

firm, whose product is considered the acme of perfection, makes nothing but actions. Most manufacturers of pianos, of the present day, build the wooden frame, the sound-board and the case only; the action, metal plate, strings, tuning-pins, etc., being purchased from different firms who make a specialty of the manufacture of these parts. A few concerns, however, make every piece that enters into the composition of the instruments bearing their names.

Ky, is the Key in its resting position.

c, wherever found, represents a cushion of felt or soft leather upon which the different parts of the action rest or come in contact with each other. Their purpose, as is readily seen, is that of rendering the action noiseless and easy of operation.

Bnc R, shows the end of the balance rail, extending the entire length of the keyboard.

B P, is the balance pin. This is a perfectly round pin driven firmly in the balance rail. The bottom of the hole in the key fits closely around the balance pin; at the top, it is the shape of a mortise, parallel with the key, which allows the key to move only in the direction intended. The mortise in the wooden cap on top of the key at this point is lined with bushing cloth which holds the key in position laterally, and prevents looseness and rattling, yet allows the key to move easily.

L, is the lead put in this portion of the key to balance it, and to insure uniformity of "touch," and quick and certain return of key to its rest position.   As there is more or less difference in the length of keys, and also in the weight of the hammers operated by them, some keys are leaded much more heavily than others.   In some cases the lead is inserted in the extreme back end of the key; in others it is put near the balance rail according to the requirement.   In some actions the lead is omitted entirely; but in the best actions it is almost invariably present.   In the action of the grand piano the keys are leaded in front of the balance rail instead of back of it.   This is due to the fact that in the grand piano the hammer rests in a horizontal position and its whole weight must be actually lifted and the force of gravity overcome, while in the upright, the hammer rests in a vertical position, only requiring to be thrown forward.

G P, is the guide pin, generally of oval shape, with the longest diameter in line with the key. The hole in the lower portion of the key, in which the guide pin works, is bushed with bushing cloth and is made to fit so closely that the key will not move laterally, yet not so tightly that the key will not work easily.

Bm, is a wooden block called the bottom; sometimes called the key-rocker. It is held in position by the two screws shown in cut by which it can be adjusted or regulated.

E, is the extension communicating the motion of the key to the upper part of the action. There are various ways in which the extension is connected to the bottom. In this action, the extension is made round at the lower end and fits snugly into a hole in the bottom upon a felt disc. When the action is taken out, the extensions simply lift out of the holes, and when it is put back it is necessary to enter each one in its place. In other actions, the upper side of the

bottom where the extension rests has no hole
but simply a felt covering upon which the extension rests; in this case it is necessary to
provide what is called an extension guide
which is hinged to the extension guide rail
shown in the cut at the left of the extension.
In actions of this kind, the extensions remain
in place at all times and the trouble of placing
them properly on the bottom when replacing
the action is obviated.   Other methods also are
employed which are readily understood upon
slight examination, but are essentially similar
to the above.   Instead of the bottom, a capstan
screw is used in some actions as follows:

Cpn, is a capstan screw used in some actions in place
of the bottom.   It is turned by inserting a
pointed instrument in one of the four holes,
thus raising or lowering the capstan in regulating.   The lower end of the extension is
felted.   In such actions the extension is invariably provided with the extension guide.

B, is the metal action bracket.   The bracket is one
solid piece of metal.   There are generally four
brackets in the upright action.   The brackets

rest on supports in and at the sides of the key-
bed, and are secured at the top by large bolts,
BB, which go through the metal plate and into
the wooden frame or pin block. At the top of
each bracket is an opening to receive this bolt
and a thumbscrew (not shown in the cut, being behind the hammer) which fastens the
action securely in position.

MR, is the main rail; so called because the main con-
stituents of the action are attached to it.
(Everything designated as "rail" in the action
runs the entire length of the action in one solid
piece.)

W, is the wippen. Those pieces upon which or by
which the small letter *g* is shown are the
flanges. The one at the left of the wippen is
called the wippen flange. It is made fast to
the main rail by a screw, and upon it the wippen is hinged by means of a "center-pin" at
the lower end. The center-pin in the wippen
is driven through a hole in which it fits tightly
and immovably in the middle part, and it (the
center-pin) is consequently stationary in the
wippen. The flange extends down at the

sides of the wippen and the holes in flange are made large enough to receive bushing cloth in which the center-pin works freely but not loosely. All flange joints are of this nature; some, however, are provided with a means for tightening the center-pin in the middle portion of the joint.

j, is the jack. The purpose of the jack is to communicate the motion of the wippen to the hammer. The precise adjustment of the jack and the adjacent parts upon which it depends for its exact movements, play an important part in regulating the "touch" of the piano, and will be fully entered into in following lessons.

js, jack spring. Its purpose is to hold the jack inward against the "nose" or "heel" of the hammer butt. (See *Bt*, hammer butt.)

Rr, regulating rail. The *regulating button* is shown attached to the rail by the regulating screw which is turned by means of its ring on top of *Rr*. The purpose of the regulating button is to throw the point of the jack out of the nose of the hammer butt, and allow the hammer to rebound from the string. If the button is too high, it does not throw or trip the jack in time to prevent blocking. When the button is too low, it disengages too soon, and much of the force of the key is lost before it reaches the hammer.

BR, is the block rail, felted on the side next to the jack which strikes against it when thrown from nose. This rail is absent in some actions, in which case the back of the jack is felted and strikes against the "back catch," which is also felted on inner side. (The back catch has no mark in the cut, but is explained below in connection with the "back check.")

BC, is the back check which is simply a piece of wood with a thick piece of felt glued to the inner face and suspended on a wire.

BCW, back check wire supporting the back check, and screwed to the wippen. The purpose of the back check is to check the hammer by coming in contact with the "back catch" (the backward projection of the butt), at a short distance from the string in its return, and prevent the hammer from falling entirely back to its rest position, thereby preventing quick repetition.

Bl, bridle. This is a piece of tape about an eighth of
an inch wide with a piece of leather glued to
the end and a hole near the end for the point of
the "stirrup" or bridle wire. The cut shows
where the bridle is fastened in the hammer
butt by being put into the hole in the butt, and
the back catch stem covered with glue and
driven in by it which precludes all possibility
of its coming loose. The bridle passes through
a hole in the lower part of the back catch. Its
purpose is to assist the hammer to return
quickly by hanging to it with the weight of the
wippen, extension, jack, etc., when the key is
released. Thus the bridle becomes the main
factor in the matter of quick repetition.

Bl W, bridle wire, screwed into wippen, bent in the
shape of a buckle at top to hold bridle.

Bt, butt; or, more specifically, hammer butt. In
some cheap actions the butt is joined to its
flange *g*, by the means described under the
head of wippen flange; but in this action the
center-pin is held firmly in the butt by a small
strip of brass containing a set screw; somewhat obscure in the cut, but discernible. As

explained elsewhere, all center-pins turn in the flange and not in the middle part.

HS, hammer shank in rest position.

H, hammer showing wood body or head, and covering of two layers of felt.

H R, hammer rail, resting on felt cushion, *c*, glued to rail or bracket. The hammer rail is held in position by the rod, shown under the hammer shank, which is hinged to the bracket at the lower end, and which allows it to be moved forward when the soft pedal is used. The soft pedal communicates with this rail by a rod which moves it forward and thereby shortens the stroke of the hammers and produces a softer tone.

sr, spring rail screwed to the brackets. This rail supports the light wire springs which assist the hammers in returning to rest position.

S, string.

D, is the damper head secured to the damper wire by a set screw.

DL, damper lever, working in damper flange *g*, which is screwed to main rail.

s, spoon; so called from its shape. It is screwed into

the wippen.   When the key is struck, the motion on the wippen throws the spoon forward, pushing the lower end of damper lever forward, and releasing the damper from its contact with the string.   The damper is held against the string by the wire spring which is seen running from the damper flange to the top of the damper lever.

DR, damper rod.   This is a rod running from the left or bass end of the action to the right as far as the dampers are continued in the treble.   It is acted upon by the "loud" or damper pedal, which raises the outer projection, and by being hinged to the main rail about the same height as this projection, the entire rod is thrown outward against the lower ends of the damper levers, releasing all the dampers simultaneously.   This being the only office of the right pedal, it is readily seen that this pedal does not increase the loudness, but simply *sustains* any number of tones struck successively, giving the effect of more volume.

The student should familiarize himself with all technical terms used in this lesson, as they will be referred to frequently in the succeeding lessons on repairing and regulating.

QUESTIONS ON LESSON III.

Without reference to anything but the cut, give technical names for parts of action represented by the following letters or abbreviations:

1. Bnc R, c, G P, BP, Ky, L.
2. Bm, Cpn, E, W, j, js, g, and M R.
3. Rr, B C, B R, B C W, Bl, and Bl W.
4. Bt, H, H S, H R, and sr.
5. S, D, D L, D R, s, B, and B B.
6. Explain the purpose and movements of the jack.
7. Describe a flange and the joint of same.
8. Give names of the four flanges shown in cut.
9. What is the purpose of the back catch and back check?
10. Explain the mechanical action of the damper pedal, and its effect when used; also, that of the soft pedal.

LESSON IV.

ACTION OF SQUARE AND GRAND PIANOS.

ACTION OF THE SQUARE PIANO.

Up to about the year 1870, the square was the popular piano. The grand has always been too expensive for the great music-loving masses, and previous to this time the upright had not been developed sufficiently to assert itself as a satisfactory instrument. The numerous objections to the square piano forced its manufacture to be discontinued a few years after the introduction of the improved new upright. Square pianos that come, at the present day, under the hand of the tuner, are usually at least fifteen years old, and more frequently twenty or more. However, in some localities the tuner will meet numbers of these pianos and he will find them a great source of revenue, as they are almost invariably in need of repair.

Compare the three cuts of actions in the study of this lesson.

The main constituent parts of the square action are similar in appearance to those of the upright; in fact, most of the parts are the same in name and office. However, the parts are necessarily assembled very differently. In the square action, the hammers strike in a vertical direction, while in the upright they strike in a horizontal direction; the motion of the key being the same in both.

Of the three types, the square is the simplest action, as many of the parts seen in the upright and grand are entirely absent in the square.

Beginning with the key, it has its balance pin, guide pin, cushions, etc., practically the same as in the other types.

The bottom, or key rocker, is reversed in the square; the end transmitting the motion being nearest the performer.

The extension and wippen are absent in the square, as the jack is attached directly to the bottom or key-rocker.

The back check is screwed to the key, and as the hammer head rests against it after striking, the use of the contrivance called the back catch in the upright is unnecessary.

The hammer rail in the square, in addition to serving its purpose as a rest for the hammers, also

Action of the Square Piano.

A. Action Frame.
B's Indicate the Cushions, or Bushing, of felt, cloth or leather.
C. Balance Rail.
D. Balance Pin.   Round.
E. Mortised Cap for Balance Pin.   Bushed.
F. Key.
G. Lead.
H. Back Check.
I. Bottom or Key Rocker.
J. Bottom Screws; used to regulate height of Jack.
K. Jack.
L. Jack Spring; concealed under Bottom.
M. Center Pin to Jack.
N. Hammer Rail.
O. Regulating Screw.
P. Regulating Button.
Q. Flange Rail.
R. Flange.   Split.
S. Flange Rail Screw.
T. Flange Screw, to regulate jaws of flange.
U. Hammer Butt.
V. Center Pin.
W. Hammer Stem or Shank.
X. Hammer Head.
Y. Hammer Felt.   Treble hammers sometimes capped with buckskin
    in old instruments.

Top Action of Square Piano.

1. Damper Lifter Wire.
2. Damper Lifter Buttons.
3. Damper Felt.
4. Damper Head.
5. Damper Lever.
6. Damper Leads.
7. Shade, supported by wire stanchions, on top of which are screwed
    shade buttons.
8. Damper Rail.   Tilted by Loud Pedal Rod which raises all the dam-
    pers simultaneously.
9. Damper Flange.
10. Flange Screw.
11. Damper Lever Center Pin.

The Trap Action

consists of Pedals, Pedal Braces, Pedal Feet, Pedal Rods, Roller Boards
or Elbows, Studs, Plugs, Trap Springs, Wires and Lifter Rods.

The cut is from the French action. Nearly all
square pianos in use at the present time are of this type.

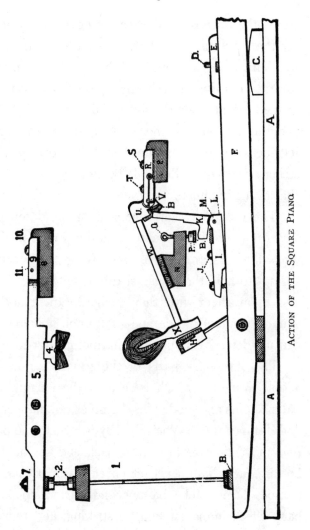

ACTION OF THE SQUARE PIANO

serves the purpose of the regulating rail, as you will see the regulating screw, with its button, attached to it.   This rail is stationary in the square, not moving toward the strings and shortening the stroke as it does in the upright when the soft pedal is used.   The soft pedal in the square piano simply interposes a piece of felt between each hammer and its corresponding string or strings.   This felt being much softer than that of the hammers, the tone is greatly subdued.

The mechanical arrangement of the dampers is very different in the square from that in the upright. The dampers are above the strings. Instead of springs to hold them against the strings, they simply rest upon them with their weight. In many old squares some of the dampers fall upon nodal points, causing defective damping or harmonic after-tones.

The stationary parts of the square action are: action frame, to which is secured the balance rail, balance pins and guide pins, hammer rail, flange rail, and damper rail.   When the key is struck, the parts that move upward are: the back end of the key, bottom, jack, hammer, back check, damper wire and damper lever.   The hammer falls back upon the back check immediately after striking, and remains there until the key is released, when all movable parts fall to rest position.

The action of the jack is the same in all types.

ACTION OF THE GRAND PIANO.

After thoroughly going over the details of the action of the square and upright pianos, there remains very little to describe in the action of the grand.

The grand action partakes of the characteristics of both the upright and the square, and is somewhat more complicated than either.

The bottom and extension are almost identical with those of the upright; the extension, however, is necessarily very short.

The wippen is of different construction, and somewhat more complicated in the grand.

The flange rail in the grand is made also to serve the purpose of regulating rail, as the hammer rail is made to do in the square.

The back check is identical with that of the square.

The dampers are the same in their working principles as those of the square, but are generally different in construction; yet, some squares have the same arrangement of dampers as those shown in the cut of the grand action.

The soft pedal of the grand shifts the entire action to the right so that the hammers strike only two and in some cases only one of the strings.

The student should study the three types of actions from the actions themselves, if possible.

INSTRUCTIONS FOR REMOVING THE SQUARE AND GRAND ACTIONS.

First, feel or look underneath the keyboard and see if there are screws that go up into the action. In most of the better grade instruments the action is

---

ACTION OF THE GRAND PIANO.

1. Indicates the felt, cloth or leather, upon which the various parts of the action rest, or fall noiselessly.
2. Key.
3. Bottom; sometimes called Key Rocker.
4. Extension; split at lower end to receive center pin in Bottom.
5. Wippen Support.
6. Jack.
7. Jack Spring.
8. Flange and Regulating Rail.
9. Regulating Screw, Button and Cushion.
10. Escapement Lever.
11. Regulating Screw in Hammer Flange, for Escapement Lever.
12. Check Wire, for Escapement Lever.
13. Screw to regulate fall of Escapement Lever.
14. Lever Flange, screwed to Flange Rail.
15. Hammer Shank.
16. Hammer.
17. Back Check.
18. Damper Lever, leaded.
19. Damper Wire, screwed into upright.
20. Damper Wire Guide, fastened to Sound-Board.
21. Damper Head and Felt.
0. Center Pins. Holes lined with Bushing Cloth.

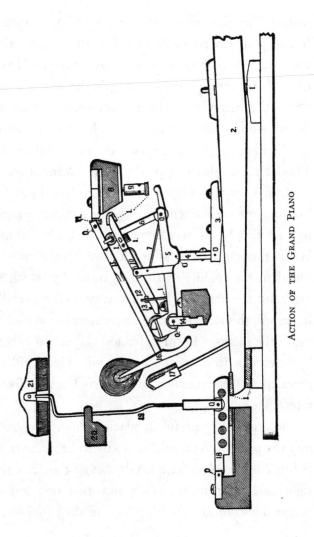

ACTION OF THE GRAND PIANO

fastened in this way. If the screws have square heads, your tuning hammer will fit them and bring them out; if common screws, a screw-driver will suffice. Look through the opening in the sound board where the hammers strike and see that they are all down before pulling out the action, lest they break off by catching on the under side of the sound board. This is almost sure to happen if actions are out of order.

In most square pianos, the narrow board just below the keys can be removed by being raised straight up, as it simply sets over screw heads in the key frame. When this strip is removed, a wire handle will be found in the middle of the key frame by which to draw out the action. In some cases, and especially in grands, this strip is secured by screws found underneath the piano. In other pianos, the action is held by screws in front of the key frame, which will be revealed by the removal of the front strip, above referred to.

Be especially careful in placing the action back into the piano. As a rule, it is safe to keep the right (long) end of the square action bearing against the right side of entrance, being sure that one end of action does not get ahead, which might cause some of the hammers to strike the props for which the openings are left in the back extremities of action.

While the action is out, study carefully the purpose of every part and its movements, referring to this and the previous lesson until you have thoroughly mastered the entire mechanism. Do not rest until you can name correctly everything you see and know its use so well that you could explain it satisfactorily to an inquirer. Sometimes the tuner is asked a great many perplexing questions and is expected to respond intelligently.

We have dealt with the three types of actions that are most commonly found in the three types of pianos. The student must bear in mind that there are numerous manufacturers of actions, and that each has his peculiar method of constructing his special action to bring about the desired results, which are practically the same in all cases; and consequently, while a variety of construction will confront the beginner in piano regulating and repairing, he will understand the construction and requirements of any action that may demand his skill from the foregoing instruction, if properly mastered. In this, as in all other mechanical professions, one's inventive genius must often be

summoned to assist in surmounting obstacles which
are sure to arise unexpectedly.

QUESTIONS ON LESSON IV.

1. From a philosophical point of view, which do you
   consider the easiest and most perfect of the
   three types of actions? Also give reasons.
2. Considering the wippen and its attachments as
   one part, how many parts move when a key is
   struck in the upright piano? How many in
   the square?
3. Name the parts found in the upright action that
   are absent in the square.
4. Describe the three methods by which soft tone is
   obtained from use of soft pedal in the three
   types of actions.
5. What rail serves two purposes in the square action, and what are they? What rail serves
   two purposes in the grand action, and what
   are they?

LESSON V.

REGULATING AND REPAIRING.

FAULTS IN PIANOS, ASIDE FROM THE ACTION, AND
THEIR REMEDIES.

One of the most common, and, at the same time,
most annoying conditions both to the owner of the
piano and the tuner, is the "sympathetic rattle."
This trouble is most usual in the square and the
grand pianos and is generally due to some loose
substance lying on the sound board. The rattle
will be apparent only when certain keys are struck,
other tones being perfectly free from it. These
tones cause the sound board to vibrate in sympathy,
so to speak, with the weight of the intruding substance at the point where it lies, and if it be moved
the distance of six inches it will sometimes cease
to respond to these particular tones, but may respond to others, or cease to cause any trouble.

The article may generally be found near the
front of the sound board under the top piece of the

case, this being the place where it would most likely fall. No special instrument is made for the purpose of searching for such objects, but one can be easily devised with which the tuner can feel all over the sound board, and remove such articles as well as dust and dirt. Secure a piece of rattan or good pliable hickory, and draw it down to the width of half an inch, thin enough to bend easily, and long enough to reach anywhere under the stringing or metal plate. By putting a cloth over this stick you can remove anything that comes in its way. Some difficulty will be found, however, in getting under the plate in some pianos. In case you cannot procure a suitable piece of wood, a piece of clock spring will be found to answer very well. We have taken from pianos such articles as pencils, pieces of candy, dolls, pointers used by music teachers, tacks, nails, pennies, buttons, pieces of broken lamp chimneys, etc., etc., any one of which is sufficient to render the piano unfit for use. The sound board of the upright being vertical prevents its being subject to the above difficulty.

A split in the sound board, in any style of piano, sometimes causes trouble due to the vibrating edges

of the board coming in contact with each other. Insert the point of your screwdriver in the crack, hold-
ing it there firmly; if the rattling stops, the difficulty
is discovered, and may be remedied by placing a
screw or wedge in the crack, or a wedge of wood,
cork or rubber between the sound board and iron
plate or casing, if the location of the trouble per-
mits. While this method seems a perfunctory one,
it is nevertheless the best the tuner is prepared to
do, for it is next to impossible to glue a crack in the
sound board successfully outside of a regular factory or repair shop, where the instrument may be
taken all apart and a new sound board put in or the
old one properly repaired.

Sometimes the sound board gets loose or unglued
at the edges, or the bridges or ribs come loose. Any
part of the piano where there is vibration or loose
material may become the source of the sympathetic
rattle, as even parts of the case vibrate with the
tones struck; so you must examine the panels, lock,
hinges, soft pedal bar (in square), in fact all parts
of the case and woodwork for the location of the
trouble. Once found, the remedy will suggest itself.
The greatest difficulty is to locate the cause. Very

frequently this will be found entirely outside of the piano; a loose window glass, picture glass, lamp or other article of furniture in the room may respond to a particular tone or its octave. We have never found the sympathetic rattle in the action; it has rattles, but not of this character. Any other defect which may be found under this head will only require the exercise of a little mechanical ingenuity to suggest a remedy.

REGULATING AND REPAIRING THE UPRIGHT ACTION.

(Use cut of upright action for reference in following study.)

We will begin with the key and take up each part of the action in the succession in which motion is transmitted.

1. *Key.*—Keys stick; that is, after being struck, they fail to come up quickly, if at all. First ascertain if the trouble is really in the key, or in the upper part of the action. To do this, lift the extension or wippen until the upper part of the action is entirely free from the key, so that you may test the key independently. Some keys are leaded so that they will fall in front of the balance rail, others so that they will fall back of it; in either case, lift the low end and let go, to see if it will fall by its own weight. If

it seems quite free, you may know the trouble is not in the key; you will also find that when you release the extension or wippen, it will not fall readily, showing that the trouble lies in the upper part.

If the trouble is found in the key, examine the guide pin. See if it is placed in a direct line with the key. If so, and it still binds, enlarge the hole by pressing the wood back slightly with some wedge-shaped instrument, if you have not a pair of the key pliers which are used for this purpose. See that the cloth, with which the hole is bushed, is not loose and wrinkled. Do not oil or grease the guide pin unless such treatment has been previously resorted to, as the polished pin will work more freely in the dry cloth. Do not pinch hard on the pin with rough pliers and spoil the polished surface.

Sometimes you will find one key warped so that it rubs on the next, in which case, plane off a slight shaving to free it. Sometimes changing the position of the guide pin will straighten or level the key and make it work all right.

The balance pin is subject to some of the same difficulties as the guide pin. See that it sets properly and is not bound by the mortise.

Sometimes a splinter will be found on one side of a key where the lead has been put in. A piece of any foreign material between two keys generally causes both to stick.

Where the action is too deep, that is, the keys go down farther than they ought, place cardboard washers under the felt ones around the guide pin, or raise the felt strip under back end of keys.

Where the action is too shallow, place thin washers under those around the balance pin. When this is done, the whole action must be regulated accordingly, as this alteration will make a change in the working of the upper part of the action.

2. *The Bottom or Capstan.*—This should be so adjusted that when the key falls back to its rest position, the point of the jack will just spring into its place in the nose of the hammer butt. If held too high, the jack fails to catch in the nose, and the key may be struck without producing any effect on the hammer. When the bottom or capstan is too low, the point of the jack will be some distance below the notch, which will cause what is known as lost motion it being necessary to depress the key a portion of its depth before the jack can act upon the

hammer. Depress the key slowly, watching the hammer, and the fault will be discovered.

After a piano has been used for some time, the keys that are struck most frequently (those in the middle of the instrument) will be found to have this fault. The felts under the keys and those which are between the working parts of the action become compressed or worn so that the jack will be found to set so low that there will be lost motion in the key. In this case, loosen one of the screws in the bottom and turn the other down so as to move the jack upward until nearly all lost motion is taken up. A little play is generally necessary, but very little. In case the action has a capstan, simply turn it upward.

3. *Back Check.*—Blocking is most usually caused by the back check being too near the back catch, so that when the key is struck, the back check holds the hammer against the string. This should be seen after raising the bottom or capstan as above referred to. It will be observed that when this is done on account of the wear of the felts, the back check will stand much nearer the back catch than it did before, and will need bending back so as to give the hammer plenty of "rebound." A steel instrument with

properly shaped notches at the point, called a regu·
lator, is used for bending wires in regulating the
action. See that the wires stand as nearly in line
as is possible. In old actions that are considerably
worn, however, you will be obliged to alter some
more than others.

4. *Bridle and Bridle Wire.*—In putting in a
new bridle, it should be doubled over at the end and
secured to the hammer butt by a small tack. Be sure
you get it exactly the same length as the others;
otherwise it will be necessary to bend the bridle wire
out of line. Some tuners glue the bridle around the
back catch stem, but the above method is preferable.

The purpose of the bridle is to jerk the hammer
back quickly and the wire must be set, neither so
far back as to check the stroke of the hammer, nor
so far forward that the bridle is too slack to draw
upon the hammer.

5. *Jack.*—The jack itself seldom gets out of
order. So long as its flange does not come unglued
in the wippen, or its spring get out of place or
broken, or get tight in its joint, it will need nothing.
Its adjustment and action is controlled by the
bottom or capstan, and the regulating button.

6. *Regulating Button.*—This button determines the point in the stroke of the hammer where the jack flies off from the nose of the butt. If the button is too high, the jack does not fly off soon enough, and the result is, that the hammer either Llocks against the string or bounces from the jack after the stroke has been made, striking the string a second or third time from one stroke of the key. The felt punching on the lower side of the button often wears until this trouble prevails. Lower the button by turning down the screw on top of the regulator rail; if lowered too far, however, the action is weakened by causing the jack to fly off too soon, without giving the hammer a sufficient impulse. A regulating screwdriver is used for this, but in its absence, a wire hook, similar to a shoe buttoner, will turn the screw.

The block rail is properly adjusted at the factory and requires no attention.

7. *Hammer Butt.*—The felts and leather on the heel of the hammer butt wear out and must be replaced. The felt cushion, that is lowest and farthest to the left (see illustration), is the one that wears out first. The jack, in returning to the notch, strikes

this cushion, and in time wears it away so that the jack in returning strikes the wood of the hammer butt, producing a sharp click, which is very annoying, to say the least. This click is heard at the instant the key rises to its rest position. Sometimes, however, a similar click is produced by the top of the key striking the board which is set over the keys, due to the cloth being eaten off by moths, or a pencil or some other article lying on the keys back of this board.

The center pin in the butt of some cheap actions is not held in the butt by metal clip and screw, and if it gets loose so that it works out, must be replaced by a larger pin. The size of center pins generally used in the factory, is .050 of an inch in diameter; the size for repairing should be .053. All of the best actions have the set screw with which to make the pin fast in the butt.

Hammers stick when the center pin is too tight in the flange. The bushing in the flange often expands. Some tuners oil at the ends of the pin with kerosene or wet it with alcohol, which is very good; but a better plan is to shrink the bushing with a drop of water on each side so that it will penetrate the bushing. After this is done, the piano cannot be used for a day or two, as the water first swells the bushing, making all the hammers stick; but when they are dry again, they will be found free. This may seem a curious method, but you need not be afraid of it; it is the most effective.

Before leaving the hammer butt, see that the hammer spring is in its place.

8. *Hammer Stem.*—These sometimes warp, split, crack, or come unglued at the butt or hammer. If twisted so far that it does not strike properly on the strings, or that it binds against the next hammer, the best thing is to put in a new stem. If merely split or unglued, it may be repaired. Sometimes a click is heard and it will seem impossible to find the cause, the hammer and stem apparently perfect, but a close examination will reveal a looseness in the stem somewhere.

In putting in a new shank, drill or chip out the old one, scrape the holes out clean, take your measure carefully, and do not make the new shank too tight, but large enough to fill the hole snugly. Apply glue to the ends of the shank and also in the holes. Cedar is used in some makes, but good maple is stronger, and is more generally used.

9. *Hammers.*—When too hard, soften with a felt pick. Do not raise the felt up, but stick the pick in the felt just back of the point and this will loosen it up and make it softer and more elastic. Where the strings have worn deep grooves, sandpaper them down nearly even and soften the felt as above.

In regluing the felt to the head, glue only the back ends of the felt, and clamp with strong rubber band till the glue sets. Use tailor's chalk (fuller's earth) to clean hammer felts. To harden or draw felts back in shape, place a damp cloth over them, and then pass a hot iron over it.

10. *Dampers.*—Damper felt often gets hardened so that when it comes against the vibrating string, it causes a sort of buzzing sound. Loosen it up with the pick. Imperfect damping can sometimes be corrected in the same way.

The damper head sometimes turns round on its wire, leaving one or two strings undamped. Tighten the set screw. See that the dampers are in line; and that they will stop the tone properly when the key is released.

Damper springs sometimes break. It is necessary to take out the damper lever to put in a new one.

See that the spoons are in line and work properly. Press the sustaining pedal down, and see if all the dampers are in line; if not, bend the damper wires with the regulator until they line up perfectly.

11. *Damper Rod.*—When the sustaining pedal squeaks, look first to the pedal, then to the wooden rods leading up to the damper rod. If the trouble is found in any of these, or the springs, use sperm oil or vaseline.

Catch hold of the damper rod at the left behind the action and work it. If it squeaks, you will have to take out the action and oil the swings where they are hinged to the main rail.

QUESTIONS ON LESSON V.

1. If you should find a key sticking, how would you determine the cause?
2. Name all the defects to which the key is subject.
3. Describe the proper adjustment of bottom or capstan.
4. Give two causes of blocking.
5. Give the purpose of the regulating button, and its proper adjustment.

LESSON VI.

REGULATING AND REPAIRING.—(Continued.)

THE SQUARE ACTION.

1. *The key* in the square piano is subject to the same troubles as that of the upright, and requires the same treatment. However, the keys being much longer are more liable to cause trouble by warping.

2. *Bottom or Key Rocker.*—Unlike in the upright action, the jack is attached directly to the bottom; but, lowering or raising the bottom has the same effect in both cases. The screws regulating the height of the jack can be gotten at with a proper screwdriver. If you have to take out the key in order to regulate the bottom, first take particular notice of the conditions in respect to the operation of the jack on the hammer. Work the key slowly, to discover if there is lost motion. Decide which way the bottom must go and how far, so that you will not have to remove and replace the key more than once

or twice to adjust it. In taking out the key, remove the board which is set edgewise over the keys immediately back of where the fingers strike, by taking out the screw at each end. Lift the hammer with the finger until the jack falls out of place; then by lifting the key off the balance pin it can be drawn out. The back check will sometimes rub so hard against the regulating button that it will be bent somewhat, and must be adjusted after the key is replaced.

The bottom is often found to have shrunken; it rattles at every stroke of the key. This can generally be stopped by simply turning the back screw down until tight, which can be done without taking the key out. This will rarely be found to alter the jack enough to cause it to fail to return to the notch in the butt. After doing this, however, it is well to examine for such a condition.

A sluggish motion of the jack is often found in old square pianos caused by the swelling of the wood, at the point where the jack is hinged to the bottom, or by the center pin's becoming foul from oxide. This will cause the jack to fail at times to operate on the hammer, especially in quick repetition. The

key is struck with no response.   Take out the bottom
entirely, and with the fingers press the sides of the
bottom inward; at the same time, work the jack back
and forth.   This will generally free it if the jack-
spring is all right.

3. *Jack.*—As in the upright, the behavior of the
jack depends entirely upon the surrounding members.   A very common occurrence in the square
piano is a broken jack-spring.   This spring is concealed in a groove on the under side of the bottom,
with a linen thread leading around the end of the
jack and held fast by a wooden plug.   If the spring
is found to be long enough, drive out the plug, attach
a new thread to the spring, and fasten as before.   If
a new spring is needed, one may be made by wrapping some small wire round a piece of music wire
of the right size.

4. *The back check, hammer stem and regulating
button* are subject to the same faults as their
counterparts in the upright, which may be remedied
in the same way.   Bridles and hammer springs
are not needed in the square, as the weight of the
hammer, moving in a vertical direction, is sufficient
to bring it to its rest position.

5. *Hammers*, when made of felt, will of course require the same treatment as those in the upright. In many old squares the hammers are built up of buckskin. If this becomes beaten down hard, it is well to cap the hammer with a new soft piece of buckskin, gluing only at the back ends.

6. *Butts and Flanges.*—A click just as the key comes up, indicates that the felt cushion, against which the jack rests, is worn out and must be replaced.

In all square actions the center pin, in the butt, is held by friction alone, but rarely gets loose; if it should be found loose, put in a larger pin.

The flange, shown in the cut, is what is called a split flange. By the set screw T, the jaws can be regulated so that they neither clamp the center pin so tightly as to make the action sluggish nor so loosely as to let the hammer wabble.

If the bushing cloth is found to be badly worn, it is better to put in new, which must be done neatly, or the result will not be satisfactory.

Hammer flanges, like all other wooden parts, shrink away from the screw heads and allow the hammer to drift to one side or rattle. While the action is in the piano, strike the keys to see if there are any that strike improperly. Mark the keys so as to indicate just what the trouble is, so that you will know how to remedy it when the action is out. If the hammers are set so close that they rub against each other, you may have to cut off a slight shaving of felt, but this is rarely necessary; for if properly placed, there is generally room for all; yet sometimes the expansion of the felt or warping of the shank makes cutting necessary.

7. *Dampers.*—The dampers in the square action depend entirely upon their weight for their efficiency in damping the strings and returning after being raised by the key. Often, after the key is struck, the damper will not return to its place and the string is undamped. This is generally found to be caused by the wire sticking in the hole through which it passes, the wire being rusty or bent or some foreign substance being in the hole round the wire. The bushing cloth in the hole may be in such condition as to retard the free passage of the damper wire, in which case the wire may be heated with a match and run up and down a few times through the hole, which will free it. The damper may not

fall readily on account of a sluggish joint in the flange. Work it back and forth as far as it will go a few times; if necessary, take it off the damper rail and look for the cause of the trouble.

Damper flanges get loose on the damper rail and work to one side, causing defective damping and rattling. See that they are all tight, and in their places.

Damper lifter buttons sometimes hold the damper off the string. See that the top button falls so low that the damper lever does not touch it when the key is released. This is accomplished by altering the lower button. Examine the damper felts to see if they are moth-eaten, or have become hardened or in any way impaired. Notice the adjustment of the shade; that it is not too low or too high. The purpose of the shade is to prevent the damper levers from flying up; but it should be high enough so that the levers do not touch it when the key is depressed gently.

Defective damping is one of the most annoying conditions, and when one is employed to regulate a piano thoroughly and put it in order, he should see that no key is left in which this occurs. Strike each

key and immediately let it up to see if it stops the
sound quickly, or, in other words, damps perfectly;
if it does not, find the cause and regulate until satisfactory.

8. *The grand action* being, in principle, practically the same as that of the square and the upright,
containing the same mechanism as is found in those
actions, it is needless to give special instructions
concerning it; as the previous work has given the
pupil a thorough knowledge of the requirements of all
actions, their common faults, and proper methods of
regulating to bring about satisfactory results. Let us
merely remark: Study thoroughly the behavior of
every component part of each action that comes
under your observation; understand what each
part is for, why it is there, and how it works or
should work properly to fill its office. Then regulate and try for results. If you have natural mechanical genius, a little experience will prepare you
to do all regulating and repairing with skill and
quickness.

Miscellaneous Repairs.

A few miscellaneous difficulties, common to all styles of actions, are occasionally met with and need to be rectified.

1. *Broken Hammer Shank.*—Glue the ends, lay a nicely fitting piece of wood, well coated with glue, on each side and wrap with binding wire. If it is broken off up so close to the hammer as not to permit this, drill a hole through the hammer head in line with the center of the shank, with a small-sized screwdriver such as watchmakers use, and run the wire through this and around the shank, drawing it firm; glue as before; when dry it will be as strong as ever. When the shank is broken off close to the butt, the same treatment will sometimes answer, but the strain here is so much greater that it is sometimes necessary to put in a new shank. In fact, it is always better to do so.

2. *Flanges, damper heads,* and all small wooden parts are liable to break or come unglued. The watchmaker's screwdriver, the binding wire and the glue must always be at hand for these emergencies. These breaks are generally in places where

wrapping is not permissible, and you are compelled to drill. Keep the screwdriver well sharpened and the drilling is easy.

3. *Ivories.*—When unglued, scrape the old glue off, apply glue to both surfaces and clamp with an ivory clamp or rubber band until the glue is firm. Apply the same treatment to ebony sharps.

4. *Leads* in the keys and the dampers of the square piano get loose and rattle. Hammer them just enough to tighten; too much might split the key.

5. *Friction.*—Where different materials, such as wood and felt, would rub together they are covered with black lead to lubricate them. The point of the jack where it comes in contact with the butt, the toe of the jack which strikes the regulating button, and the long wooden capstan which takes the place of the extension and works directly on the under side of the wippen, which is covered with felt, are black-leaded. When a key squeaks and goes down reluctantly, the trouble can usually be traced to these places; especially to the wooden capstan, the black lead having worn away. Use powdered black lead on these parts.

There are many things in this kind of work that require only the exercise of "common sense." These we have omitted to mention, treating only of those things the student does not know intuitively.

QUESTIONS ON LESSON VI.

1. When a key snaps or clicks at the instant it is let up, give two or more conditions that might cause it.

2. When a key simply rattles, what parts of the action would you examine for the trouble?

3. When a key is struck and there is no response, what may be the cause?

4. Give two causes for defective damping in a square piano.

5. Give cause of and remedy for a squeaking key.

LESSON VII.

THE STUDY AND PRACTICE OF PIANO TUNING.

Before commencing the systematic study of piano tuning, we want to impress the student with a few important facts that underlie the great principles of scale building and general details of the art.

If you have followed the suggestions, and thoroughly mastered the work up to this point you should now have some idea of the natural and artificial phenomena of musical tones; you should have a clear knowledge at least of the fundamental principles of harmony and the technical terms by which we designate intervals and their relation to each other; a knowledge of the general and specific construction of the different types of pianos and their actions, and the methods employed to put them in perfect working condition mechanically. This admitted, we are ready to consider the art of tuning—

one, the appreciation of which is in direct proportion to the understanding of it.   Let us now view this art for a moment in its past, present and future phases.

You may be a little surprised at what we are about to tell you, but it is a fact, gleaned from long experience in traveling and observation, that many, verily, the majority of pretending tuners have not so much practical knowledge of a piano as you should now have.   We have no doubt that you, if you have a musical ear, could, without further instruction, improve an instrument that was extremely out of tune.   You could detect and improve a tone which you should find extremely sharp or flat; you could detect and improve a unison that might be badly out, and you might produce an entire scale in which none of the chords would be unbearably rasping. But this is not enough.   You should aspire to perfection, and not stop short of it.

It may seem to us who are musicians with thorough knowledge of the simpler laws of music, that a scale of eight tones is a simple affair; simply a natural consequence; the inevitable arrangement; but a historical investigation will prove our mistake.   We will not go into the complexities of musical history; suffice it to say that the wisest philosophers who lived prior to the fourteenth century had no idea of a scale like that we have at the present day.

In piano tuning, as in other arts, many theories and conjectures have been advanced regarding the end to be sought and the means by which to gain it. There must be a plan—a system by which to work. The question is: What plan will insure the most perfect results with the least amount of labor? In Piano Tuning, this plan is called the Temperament.

Webster defines the word thus: "A system of compromises in the tuning of pianofortes, organs," etc. Later on we will discuss fully what these compromises are, and why they exist; for it is in them that the tuner demonstrates his greatest skill, and to them that the piano owes its surpassing excellence as a musical instrument, and, consequently, its immense popularity. For the present, the term "temperament" may be considered as meaning the plan or pattern from which the tuner works.

No subject of so great importance in the whole realm of musical science has been so strangely neglected as the method of setting a temperament.

Even musicians of high learning, in other respects, give little attention to scale building, and hence they differ widely on this topic.   There can be but one "best way" of doing a thing, and that best way should be known and followed by the profession; but, strange to say, there are a half dozen systems of setting the temperament in vogue at the present time.   The author has, in his library, a book on "Temperament" which, if followed, would result in the production of a scale in which every chord would be unbalanced, harsh and unbearable.   This is mentioned merely to call attention to the fact that great differences of opinion exist among scientific men regarding this important subject.

In the author's practice, he was curious to try the different methods, and has tuned by all the systems of temperament in vogue at the present, or that have ever been used extensively.   His experience has proved that all but one is hampered with uncertainty, difficulty of execution or imperfection in some respect.

A system which will positively insure the strictest uniformity of difference in pitch of any given interval in all the keys, and that makes use of the fewest intervals in tuning and the easiest ones—those in which a discrepancy is most readily perceived by the ear, is the best system to adopt and follow. Such a system is the one followed by the author for years with the most satisfying results. He does not claim any high honor by this statement, but does claim that, while his system differs but slightly from some of the others, it is more certain to produce the best results, is the simplest to understand, is the easiest to follow, and, consequently, is the best.

To become a piano tuner of the highest skill, many things are necessary; but what may be lacking at the outset may be acquired by study and practice. More depends upon the ear than upon anything else; but no person, however talented, has a sufficiently acute perception to tune perfectly without some culture. Some practice in tuning is necessary to bring the ear to that acuteness of perception so indispensable in certain portions of the instrument. It may also be said that no extraordinary talent for music is absolutely necessary, since many of the best tuners are not musicians in any sense of the word. Patience and perseverance, associated with conscientiousness and an insatiable desire to excel, are among the foremost requirements.   Having these it only remains to gain a thorough knowledge of every detail of the work; a little practice will bring skill and dexterity.

Finally, we would impress the student with the strenuous importance of thoroughly mastering the lessons which immediately follow.   You should be inspired with the utmost confidence, both in yourself and in the possibilities of the profession to those who merit a reputation.   And, while this lesson contains little technical instruction, if by its study the pupil is impressed with the maxims herein presented, and is inspired to make earnest effort in his future work, both in acquiring and in practicing the art of Piano Tuning, the author will feel that its mission is, by no means, the least significant one in the course.

LESSON VIII.

THE TEMPERAMENT.

Some tuners favor the term, "laying the bearings," others say "setting the temperament." The former is more commonplace, as it merely suggests the idea of laying a number of patterns by which all others are to be measured. The latter term is extremely comprehensive. A lucid definition of the word "temperament," in the sense in which it is used here, would require a discourse of considerable length. The following statements will elicit the full meaning of the term:

The untutored would, perhaps, not think of setting a temperament to tune by. He would likely begin at some unfavorable point, and tune by various intervals, relying wholly upon his conception of pitch for the accuracy of the tones tuned, the same as a violinist in tuning his four strings. To be sure, pitch has to be reckoned as a rude guide in setting the tones; but if pitch alone were the guide we would never attain to any degree of perfection in scale forming. We could never adjust our tones to that delicate fineness so much appreciated, which gives to the instrument its surpassing brilliancy.

Beats, Waves, Pulsations.—To obtain absolute accuracy the tuner is guided by beats, waves or pulsations. These three words refer to one and the same thing, a phenomenon that occurs in certain intervals when two tones are sounded together that are not in exact tune. These terms must not be confounded with the term "sound wave" or "vibrations" so often used in discussions on the theory of sound. However, we think the student is thoroughly familiar with these terms. The rate of vibration of two tones not in a favorable ratio, may produce the phenomenon known as "beats, waves, or pulsations." Vibrations may exist either with or without pulsations.

These pulsations are most perceptible in the unison, the octave and the fifth. They are more easily perceived in the unison than in the octave, and more easily in the octave than in the fifth. They are also perceptible in the perfect fourth, the major and minor third and some other intervals, but on account of their obscurity, and because these intervals are unnecessary in tuning they have long since been abandoned in "temperament making" (with the exception of the perfect fourth) by most tuners, although a few still make use of it. We do not say that the fourth is unsafe to tune by, but you will see later on why it is not best to make use of it.

The Fischer System or method of "setting the temperament" has these advantages: It uses but two kinds of intervals: the fifth and octave; by employing two whole octaves in place of one or one and a half, nearly all of the middle section of strings is brought up in pitch which insures that the temperament will stand better while the remaining strings are being tuned; and the alternate tuning of the fifth and octave makes the system exceedingly easy to learn, enabling the tuner to work with less mental strain. Also the two-octave system gives a greater compass for testing, thus insuring greater accuracy.

If you have access to a piano, it will now be well for you to begin training the ear to perceive the pulsations. If you cannot use a piano, you can train very well by the use of a mandolin, guitar, violin, zither, or any stringed instrument. An instrument with metal strings, however, is better, as the vibrations are more perfect.

You will, of course, know that the front top panel of the case has to be removed to give access to the tuning pins, and that you should have a regular tuning hammer and set of mutes to begin with. The panel is held in place in various ways: sometimes with buttons, sometimes with pins set in slots, and sometimes with patent fastenings; but a little examination will reveal how it may be removed.

To produce a tone of a certain pitch, the string must be of the right thickness and length. These items are decided by the scale draughtsman in the factory; if incorrect, the tuner can do nothing to improve them.

To produce the correct pitch, the string must be of the right tension, which is brought about by winding one end of the string around the tuning pin until the proper degree of tension is reached. This must be decided by the ear of the tuner. Two strings of equal thickness and equal length produce the same tone when brought to the same tension; the result being known as "unison." A defect in the unison being the easiest way in which to detect the beats, we advise that the student practice on it first.

After taking out the panel, the first thing to do is to place your rubber mute between two trios of strings (if the piano is an upright which usually has three strings to a note) so that only two strings sound when the key is struck. Select some key near the middle of the keyboard. Strike the key strongly and hold it down. If the two sounding strings give forth a smooth, unwavering tone—a tone that sounds as if it came from one string, the unison is perfect. If you find it so, remove the mute and place it on the other side of the trio of strings. If the piano has been tuned recently by an expert, you may have to continue your search over several keys before you find an imperfect unison; but you will rarely find a piano in such perfect tune that it will not contain some defective unisons. However, if you do not succeed in finding a defective unison, select a key near the middle of the key-board, place your mute so that but two strings sound, and with your tuning hammer loosen one of the strings very slightly. Now you will notice a throbbing, beating sound, very unlike the tone produced when the strings were in exact unison. See if you can count the beats. If you have lowered the tension too much, the beats will be too rapid to permit counting. Now with a steady and gradual pull, with the heel of the hand against some stationary part, bring the string up slowly. You will notice these waves become slower and slower. When they become quite slow, stop and count, or wave the hand in time with the pulsations. After practicing this until you are sure your ear has become accustomed to the beats and will recognize them again, you may proceed to perfect the unison. Bring the string up gradually as before, and when the unison is reached you will hear one single, simple, musical tone, as though it were from a single string. Never have more than two strings sounding at once. You might go over the entire key-board now and correct all the unisons if the scale is yet fairly good. See which string is, in your opinion, the nearest to correctness with respect to the scale, and tune the other one, or two, as the case may be, to it. If the scale is badly out of symmetry, you will not get very good results without setting a temperament; but the tones will sound better individually. This experiment is more for practice than for improving the piano.

The cause of the waves in a defective unison is the alternate recurring of the periods when the condensations and rarefactions correspond in the two strings and then antagonize. This is known in physics as "interference of sound-waves."

The Octave.—When perfectly tuned, the upper tone of the octave has exactly double the number of vibrations of the lower. If the lower tone vibrates 1000 per second, the upper will vibrate 2000. Of course, the ear cannot ascertain in any way the number of vibrations per second; we use these figures for scientific demonstration only. However, there is an instrument called the Siren which is constructed for the purpose of ascertaining the number of vibrations per second of any given tone, and which is delicately accurate in its work. By its assistance we know, definitely, a great many things regarding our musical scale of which we would otherwise be ignorant. But, while we cannot, by the ear, ascertain these numbers, we can, by the "interference of sound-waves" above referred to, ascertain, to the most delicate point, when the relative vibration of two strings is mathematically exact, if they are tuned to a unison, octave, fifth, etc.

Practice now on tuning the octave. Find an octave in which the upper tone is flat. Mute all but one string in the lower tone to make sure of getting a pure tone, then select one string (the middle one if a piano has three strings) of the upper octave and proceed to pull it up gradually until all beats disappear. This being done, bring up the unisons.

The Fifth.—In our system, when we speak of a fifth, we mean a fifth upward. The fifth to C is G, to G is D, and so on.

The vibration of the fifth is one and a half times that of its fundamental. If a certain F vibrates 100, the C, a fifth above, will vibrate 150, if tuned so that no waves are heard; but for reasons which will be fully explained later, the fifth cannot be tuned with mathematical precision. On account of certain peculiarities in our tempered scale, the fifth must always be left somewhat flatter than perfect. This fact is always learned with some astonishment by beginners.

In your practice on tuning the fifth, first tune it perfectly, so that no waves are perceptible; then flat it so that there are very slow waves; less than one per second. Some authorities say there should be three beats in five seconds; but the tuner must learn to determine this by his own judgment. The tempering of the fifth will be treated exhaustively in subsequent lessons.

We advise that you confine your practice to the unison until you are sure you have a clear conception of its peculiarities in all portions of the key-board, except the extreme lower and upper octaves; do not try these yet. Do not begin to practice on the octave until you are very familiar with the beats in the unison. By gradual progress you will avoid confusing the ear, each step being thoroughly mastered before advancing to the next. Remember, there is nothing that is extremely difficult in learning to tune if you but understand what has to be done, go about it systematically, and have plenty of patience.

In this lesson we give you our system of setting the temperament; that is, the succession in which the different tones of the temperament are tuned. We advise, however, that you do not attempt to set a temperament until after studying Lesson IX, which enters into the theory of temperament, testing, etc.

Two octaves are used for the temperament: an octave above, and an octave below middle C. Middle C can be told by its being the C nearest the name

of the piano on the name board. In other words, it
is the fifth C from the highest C, and the fourth from
the lowest in the modern piano, which has seven and
a third octaves.

The diagram illustrates the two octaves of the
key-board, and shows how each key is designated in
giving the system of temperament.

Pitch.—The Piano Manufacturers' Association
has established what is known as "international
pitch." Tuning-forks made to this pitch are marked
"C–517.3," meaning that our 3C vibrates 517.3 per
second. Concert pitch is nearly a half step higher than
this. Some manufacturers still tune their instruments to this higher pitch.

If it is desired to tune a piano to a certain pitch,
say concert pitch, tune the C that is an octave above
middle C by a concert pitch tuning-fork or pipe.
If, however, the piano is too much below that, it is
not safe to bring it up to it at one tuning. But, say
it will permit tuning to concert pitch; after this C
(3C) is well laid, tune middle C (2C) by it, then tune
the C octave below middle C (1C) to middle C.
Having 1C for a starting point, proceed by tuning
a fifth up, then its octave, then a fifth, then an

octave, always tuning the octave whichever way is necessary to keep within the two octaves.

The simplicity of this system can be readily seen; yet for the use of beginners, we give on the following page the whole succession of intervals as they are taken in setting the temperament.

DIAGRAM OF THE TWO OCTAVES USED IN "TEMPERAMENT," AND OF THE SUCCESSION IN WHICH THEY ARE TUNED.

```
   C# D#    F# G# A#      C# D#    F# G# A#
C  D  E  F  G  A  B    C  D  E  F  G  A  B  C
                       *
1C, 1D, 1E, etc. _____ 2C, 2D, 2E, etc. _____ 3C
```

Middle C begins second octave; known by the asterisk (*) under it.

THE FISCHER SYSTEM OF SETTING TEMPERAMENT.

First, tune 3C by tuning pipe, or as directed.

By this, tune 2C, and by 2C tune 1C; then tune as follows:

By 1C	tune	1G	fifth above,
" 1G	"	2G	octave above,
" 1G	"	2D	fifth above,
" 2D	"	1D	octave below,

By	1D	tune	1A	fifth above,
"	1A	"	2A	octave above,
"	1A	"	2E	fifth above,
"	2E	"	1E	octave below,
"	1E	"	1B	fifth above,
"	1B	"	2B	octave above,
"	1B	"	2F♯	fifth above,
"	2F♯	"	1F♯	octave below,
"	1F♯	"	2C♯	fifth above,
"	2C♯	"	1C♯	octave below,
"	1C♯	"	1G♯	fifth above,
"	1G♯	"	2G♯	octave above,
"	1G♯	"	2D♯	fifth above,
"	2D♯	"	1D♯	octave below,
"	1D♯	"	1A♯	fifth above,
"	1A♯	"	2A♯	octave above,
"	1A♯(B♭)	"	2F	fifth above,
"	2F	"	1F	octave below,
"	1F	try	2C	fifth above.

You will observe this last fifth brings you back to the starting-point (C). It is called the "wolf," from the howling of its beats when the tuner has been inaccurate or the piano fails to stand.

QUESTIONS ON LESSON VIII.

1. What is the cause of the beats or pulsations?
2. Have you practiced tuning the unison?

3. Can you distinguish the beats clearly?
4. Have you practiced tuning the octave?
5. Do you thoroughly understand the system of setting the temperament as set forth in this lesson?

LESSON IX.

SPECIFIC INSTRUCTIONS IN TEMPERAMENT SETTING.

Pitch.—It is a matter of importance in tuning an instrument that it be tuned to a pitch that will adapt it to the special use to which it may be subjected. As previously explained, there are at present two different pitches in use, international pitch and concert pitch, the latter being about a half-step higher than the former. The tuner should carry with him a tuning pipe or fork tuned to 3C in one or the other of these pitches. The special uses to which pianos are subjected are as follows:

1st, As a concert piano.—In the opera house, music hall, and occasionally in the church, or even in a private dwelling, the piano is used along with orchestral instruments. All orchestral instruments are supposed to be tuned to concert pitch. The stringed instruments can, of course, be tuned to any pitch; but the brass and wood-wind instruments are not so adjustable. The brass instruments are provided with a tuning slide and their pitch can be lowered somewhat, but rarely as much as a half-step, while the clarinet should not be varied from its fixed pitch if it can be avoided. It is desirable, then, that all pianos used with orchestra should be tuned to concert pitch if possible.

2d, As an accompaniment for singing.—Some persons use their pianos mainly for accompanying. It may be that singers cannot sing high, in which case they are better pleased if the piano is tuned to international pitch, while others, especially concert singers, have their pianos at a higher pitch. Where a piano is used in the home to practice by, and the singer goes out to various places to sing with other instruments, we have always advised to have the piano tuned as near concert pitch as it would bear, for the reason that if one practices with an instrument tuned to concert pitch he may feel sure of reaching the pitch of any instrument he may be called upon to sing with elsewhere.

The great majority of pianos are left entirely to the tuner's judgment in regard to pitch. The tuner knows, or should know, to what pitch to tune the piano to insure the best results. The following suggestions will be found entirely safe to follow in deciding the question of the pitch to which to tune:

Ascertain if the piano is used with orchestra, and if clarinets and cornets are used. If so, and the piano is not too much below concert pitch, and bids fair to stand the tension, draw your 3C up to concert pitch and proceed to lay your temperament. If the piano is nearly as low as international pitch, do not try to bring it up at one tuning to concert unless the owner demands it, when you may explain that it will not stand in tune long. The slightest alteration possible, in the pitch of an instrument, insures the best results, so far as standing in tune is concerned.

If everything be left to your judgment, as it generally is, and the instrument is for general, rather than special use, set your temperament at such a pitch as will require the least possible alteration. This may be arrived at in the following way: Ascertain which portion of the instrument has fallen the most. The overstrung bass strings generally stand better than any other, and in most cases you will find the C which is two octaves below middle C

to be higher (relatively) than any other C in the
piano. If so, take it as a basis and tune by perfect
octaves up to 3C.

The supposition is, that all strings in an instrument gradually grow flatter; and in a well-balanced
instrument they should do so; but the fact is, that
in certain cases some of the strings will grow sharper.
The cause is this: The tension of the strings on one
side of a brace in the metal plate or frame is greater
than on the other side; and if there is any yielding
of the structure, the result is that the overpowered
strings are drawn tighter. This condition, however,
is rare in the better grade of pianos. Here is a rule
which is safe, and will prove satisfactory in ninety-
nine per cent. of your practice where no specific
pitch is prescribed:

Take the three Cs included in the temperament
and the C that is an octave below 1C, and try each
of them with its octave until you ascertain which is
the sharpest with respect to the others; then, bring
the others up to it. You now have your pitch
established in the Cs and can begin on 1C and proceed to set the temperament. Before applying this
rule, it is well to try 3C with tuning pipe or fork to

see if the piano is below international pitch. We would not advise tuning any modern piano below international pitch. Aim to keep within the bounds of the two prescribed pitches; never higher than concert, nor lower than international. If, however, you should be called on to tune an old instrument that has become extremely low, with very rusty strings, and perhaps with some of them broken, that by all appearances will not stand even international pitch, you may be compelled to leave it somewhat below.

The Continuous Mute.—Do not try to set a temperament without a continuous mute. Its purpose is to mute all outside (1st and 3d*) strings of all the trios included in the temperament so that none but the middle strings sound when struck by the hammers. The advantage of this can be seen at once. The tuner tunes only the middle strings in setting the temperament and thereby avoids the confusion of hearing more than two strings at once. The continuous mute is then removed and the outside strings tuned to the middle. Without the continuous

---

* The three strings composing the trio or unison are numbered 1st, 2d or middle, and 3d, from left to right.

mute, he would be obliged to tune all three of the strings of the unison before he could tune another interval by it, and it would not be so safe to tune by as a single string, as there might be a slight discrepancy in the unison giving rise to waves which would confuse the ear. The tuner should hear but two strings at once while setting a temperament; the one he is tuning by and the one he is tuning. A continuous mute is a strip of muting felt of the proper thickness to be pushed in between the trios of strings. Simply lay it across a portion of the strings and with a screwdriver push it in between the trios just above where the hammers strike. In the square piano, which has but two strings to a key, the continuous mute cannot be used and you will be obliged to tune both strings in unison before leaving to tune another interval. This is one of the reasons why the square piano does not, as a rule, admit of as fine tuning as the upright.

It is presumed that you are now familiar with the succession of tones and intervals used in setting the temperament. Fix these things in your mind and the system is easy to understand and remember. Keep within the bounds of the two octaves laid out in Lesson X. Tune all fifths upward; that is, tune all fifths by their fundamentals. For example, starting on 1C, use it as fundamental, and by it, tune its fifth, which is G; then, having G tuned, use it as fundamental, and by it tune its fifth, which is D, and so on through. After tuning a fifth, always tune its octave either above or below, whichever way it lies within the bounds of the two octaves. After going through one or two experiments in setting temperament you will see the simplicity of this system and will, perhaps, not be obliged to refer to the diagram any more.

For various reasons, it is better to try your experiments on an upright piano, and the better the piano, the more satisfactory will be the result of the experiment. You should have no hesitancy or timidity in taking hold of a good piano, as you cannot damage it if you use good judgment, follow instructions, and work carefully. The first caution is, be very careful that you draw a string but slightly sharper than it is to be left. Rest the heel of the hand against some stationary part of the piano and pull very slowly, and in a direct right angle with the tuning pin so as to avoid any tendency to bend or spring the pin. We would advise now that you find an upright piano that is badly out of tune, if you have none of your own, and proceed to set a temperament.

The following instructions will suffice for your first experiments, and by them you may be able to get fairly good results; however, the theory of temperament, which is more thoroughly entered into in Lesson XII, must be studied before you can have a thorough understanding of the causes and effects.

After deciding, as per instructions on pitch which C you will tune first, place the tuning hammer (using the star head if pins are square) on the pin with the handle extending upwards or inclined slightly to the right. (The star head, which will fit the pin at eight different angles, enables the tuner to select the most favorable position.) To raise the pitch, you will, of course, pull the hammer to the right. In order to make a string stand in tune, it is well to draw it very slightly above the pitch at which it is to remain, and settle it back by striking the key repeatedly and strongly, and at the same time bearing gently to the left on the tuning hammer. The exact amount of over-tension must be learned by practice;

but it should be so slight as to be barely perceptible. Aim to get the string tuned with the least possible turning of the hammer. The tension of the string should be evenly distributed over its entire length; that is, over its vibrating middle and its "dead ends" beyond the bridges. Therefore it is necessary to strike the key strongly while tuning so as to make the string draw through the bridges. By practice, you will gain control of the hammer and become so expert that you can feel the strings draw through the bridges and the pins turn in the block.

Having now tuned your three Cs, you will take 1C as a starting point, and by it, tune 1G a perfect fifth above. Tune it perfect by drawing it gradually up or down until all pulsations disappear. Now after making sure you have it perfect, flatten it until you can hear slow, almost imperceptible waves; less rapid than one per second. This flattening of the fifth is called tempering, and from it comes the word "temperament." The fact that the fifth must always be tuned a little flatter than perfect, is a matter which always causes some astonishment when first learned. It seems, to the uninitiated, that every interval should be made perfect; but it is impossible to make them so, and get a correct scale, as we shall see later on.

Now tune 2G by the 1G just tuned, to a perfect octave. Remember that all octaves should be left perfect—all waves tuned out. Now try 2G with 2C. If your octaves are perfect, this upper fifth will beat a little faster than the lower one, but the dissonance should not be so great as to be disagreeable. Proceed to your next fifth, which is 2D, then its octave, 1D, then its fifth and so on as per directions on the system card. You can make no chord trials until you have tuned E, an interval of a major third from C.

Having tuned 2E, you can now make your first trial: the chord of C. If you have tempered your fifths correctly, this chord will come out in pleasing harmony, and yet the E will be somewhat sharper than a perfect major third to C. Now, just for experiment, lower 2E until all waves disappear when sounded with 2C. You now have a perfect major third. Upon sounding the chord, you will find it more pleasing than before; but you cannot leave your thirds perfect. Draw it up again to its proper temperament with A, and you will notice it has very

pronounced beats when sounded with C. Proceed
with the next step, which is that of tuning 1B, fifth
to 1E. When tuned, try it as a major third in the
chord of G. At each step from this on, try the note
just tuned as a major third in its proper chord. Remember, the third always sounds better if lower
than you dare to leave it; but, on the other hand, it
must not be left so sharp as to be at all unpleasant
when heard in the chord. As to the position of the
chord for these trials, the second position, that is,
with the third the highest, is the most favorable, as
in this position you can more easily discern excessive
sharpness of the third, which is the most common
occurrence. When you have gone through the entire
system and arrived at the last fifth, 1F–2C, you should
find it nearly as perfect as the rest, but you will hardly
be able to do so in your first efforts. Even old tuners
frequently have to go over their work a second or
third time before all fifths are properly tempered. By
this system, however, you cannot go far wrong if
you test each step as directed, and your first chord
comes up right. If the first test, G–C–E, proves
that there is a false member in the chord, do not proceed with the system, but go over the first seven steps

until you find the offending members and rectify. Do not be discouraged on account of failures. No one ever set a correct temperament at the first attempt.

QUESTIONS ON LESSON IX.

1. Define the terms, "International Pitch," and "Concert Pitch."

2. How would you arrive at the most favorable pitch at which to tune a piano, if the owner did not suggest any certain pitch ?

3. What is the advantage in using the continuous mute ?

4. Tell what is necessary in the tuning of a string to insure it to stand well ?

5. What would result in the major third C–E, if all the fifths, up to E, were tuned perfect ?

LESSON X.

THEORY OF THE TEMPERAMENT.

The instructions given in Lessons VIII and IX cover the subject of temperament pretty thoroughly in a way, and by them alone, the student might learn to set a temperament satisfactorily; but the student who is ambitious and enthusiastic is not content with a mere knowledge of how to do a thing; he wants to know why he does it; why certain causes produce certain effects; why this and that is necessary, etc. In the following lessons we set forth a comprehensive demonstration of the theory of Temperament, requirements of the correct scale and the essentials of its mathematics.

Equal Temperament.—Equal temperament is one in which the twelve fixed tones of the chromatic scale* are equidistant. Any chord will be as harmonious in one key as in another.

---

* The chromatic scale is a succession of all the half steps in the compass of one octave. Counting the octave tone, it contains thirteen tones, but we speak of twelve, as there are only twelve which differ in name.

Unequal Temperament.—Unequal temperament was practiced in olden times when music did not wander far from a few keys which were favored in the tuning. You will see, presently, how a temperament could be set in such a way as to favor a certain key (family of tones) and also those keys which are nearly related to it; but, that in favoring these keys, our scale must be constructed greatly to the detriment of the "remote" keys. While a chord or progression of chords would sound extremely harmonious in the favored keys, they would be so unbalanced in the remote keys as to render them extremely unpleasant and almost unfit to be used. In this day, when piano and organ music is written and played in all the keys, the unequal temperament is, of course, out of the question. But, strange to say, it is only within the last half century that the system of equal temperament has been universally adopted, and some tuners, even now, will try to favor the flat keys because they are used more by the mass of players who play little but popular music, which is mostly written in keys having flats in the signature.

Upon the system table you will notice that the first five tones tuned (not counting the octaves) are

C, G, D, A and E; it being necessary to go over these fifths before we can make any tests of the complete major chord or even the major third. Now, just for a proof of what has been said about the necessity of flattening the fifths, try tuning all these fifths perfect. Tune them so that there are absolutely no waves in any of them and you will find that, on trying the chord G–C–E, or the major third C–E, the E will be very much too sharp. Now, let your E down until perfect with C, all waves disappearing. You now have the most perfect, sweetest harmony in the chord of C (G, C, E) that can be produced; all its members being absolutely perfect; not a wave to mar its serene purity. But, now, upon sounding this E with the A below it, you will find it so flat that the dissonance is unbearable. Try the minor chord of A (A–C–E) and you will hear the rasping, throbbing beats of the too greatly flattened fifth.

So, you see, we are confronted with a difficulty. If we tune our fifths perfect (in which case our fourths would also be perfect), our thirds are so sharp that the ear will not tolerate them; and, if we tune our thirds low enough to banish all beats, our fifths are intolerably flat.

The experiment above shows us beautifully the prominent inconsistency of our scale. We have demonstrated, that if we tune the members of the chord of C so as to get absolutely pure harmony, we could not use the chord of A on account of the flat fifth E, which did duty so perfectly as third in the chord of C.

There is but one solution to this problem: Since we cannot tune either the fifth or the third perfect, we must compromise, we must strike the happy medium. So we will proceed by a method that will leave our fifths flatter than perfect, but not so much as to make them at all displeasing, and that will leave our thirds sharper than perfect, but not intolerably so.

We have, thus far, spoken only of the octave, fifth and third. The inquisitive student may, at this juncture, want to know something about the various other intervals, such as the minor third, the major and minor sixth, the diminished seventh, etc. But please bear in mind that there are many peculiarities in the tempered scale, and we are going to have you fully and explicitly informed on every point, if you will be content to absorb as little at a time as you are prepared to receive. While it may seem to us that the tempered scale is a very complex institution when viewed as a specific arrangement of tones from which we are to derive all the various kinds of harmony, yet, when we consider that the chromatic scale is simply a series of twelve half-steps—twelve perfectly similar intervals—it seems very simple.

Bear in mind that the two cardinal points of the system of tuning are:

1. All octaves shall be tuned perfect.

2. All fifths shall be tuned a little flatter than perfect.

You have seen from Lesson VIII that by this system we begin upon a certain tone and by a circle of twelve fifths cover every chromatic tone of the scale, and that we are finally brought around to a fifth, landing upon the tone upon which we started.

So you see there is very little to remember. Later on we will speak of the various other intervals used in harmony: not that they form any prominent part in scale forming, for they do not; but for the purpose of giving the learner a thorough understanding of all that pertains to the establishing of a correct equal temperament.

If the instruction thus far is understood and carried out, and the student can properly tune fifths and octaves, the other intervals will take care of themselves, and will take their places gracefully in any harmony in which they are called upon to take part; but if there is a single instance in which an octave or a fifth is allowed to remain untrue or untempered, one or more chords will show it up. It may manifest itself in one chord only. A tone may be untrue to our tempered scale, and yet sound beautifully in certain chords, but there will always be at least one in which it will "howl." For instance, if in the seventh step of our system, we tune E a little too flat, it sounds all the better when used as third in the chord of C, as we have shown in the experiment mentioned on page 94 of this lesson. But, if the remainder of the temperament is accurate, this E, in the chord in which E acts as tonic or fundamental, will be found to be too flat, and its third, G sharp, will demonstrate the fact by sounding too sharp.

The following suggestions will serve you greatly in testing: When a third sounds disagreeably sharp, one or more fifths have not been sufficiently flattened.*

---

*In making these suggestions, no calculation is made for the liability

While it is true that thirds are tuned sharp, there is a limit beyond which we cannot go, and this excessive sharpness of the third is the thing that tuners always listen for.

The fundamental sounds better to the ear when too sharp. The reason for this is the same as has already been explained above; namely, if the fundamental is too sharp the third will be less sharp to it, and, therefore, nearer perfect.

After you have gone all over your temperament, test every member of the chromatic scale as a fundamental of a chord, as a third, and as a fifth. For instance: try middle C as fundamental in the chord of C (G–C–E or E–G–C or C–E–G). Then try it as third in the chord A flat (E flat–A flat–C or C–E flat–A flat or A flat–C–E flat). Then try it as fifth in the chord of F (C–F–A or A–C–F or F–A–C). Take G likewise and try it as fundamental in the chord of G in its three positions, then try it as a

---

of the tones tuned to fall. This often happens, in which case your first test will display a sharp third. In cases like this it is best to go on through, taking pains to temper carefully, and go all over the temperament again, giving all the strings an equal chance to fall. If the piano is very bad, you may have to bring up the unisons roughly, inuring this portion of the instrument to the increased tension, when you may again place your continuous mute and set your temperament with more certainty.

third in the chord of E flat, then as fifth in the chord of C. In like manner try every tone in this way, and if there is a falsely tempered interval in the scale you will be sure to find it.

You now understand that the correctness of your temperament depends entirely upon your ability to judge the degree of flatness of your fifths; provided, of course, that the strings stand as tuned. We have told you something about this, but you may not be able at once to judge with sufficient accuracy to insure a good temperament. Now, we have said, let the fifths beat a little more slowly than once a second; but the question crops up, How am I to judge of a second of time? The fact is that a second of time is quickly learned and more easily estimated, perhaps, than any other interval of time; however, we describe here a little device which will accustom one to estimate it very accurately in a short time. The pendulum oscillates by an invariable law which says that a pendulum of a certain length will vibrate always in a corresponding period of time, whether it swings through a short arc or a long one. A pendulum thirty-nine and a half inches long will vibrate seconds by a single swing; one nine and seven-eighths inches long will vibrate seconds at the double swing, or the to-and-fro swing. You can easily make one by tying any little heavy article to a string of either of these lengths. Measure from the center of such heavy article to the point of contact of the string at the top with some stationary object. This is a sure guide. Set the pendulum swinging and count the vibrations and you will soon become quite infallible. Having acquired the ability to judge a second of time you can go to work with more confidence.

Now, as a matter of fact, in a scale which is equally tempered, no two fifths beat exactly alike, as the lower a fifth, the slower it should beat, and thus the fifths in the bass are hardly perceptibly flat, while those in the treble beat more rapidly. For example, if a certain fifth beat once a second, the fifth an octave higher will beat twice a second, and one that is two octaves higher will beat four times a second, and so on, doubling the number of beats with each ascending octave.

In a subsequent lesson, in which we give the mathematics of the temperament, these various ratios will be found accurately figured out; but for the present let us notice the difference between the actual tempered scale and the exact mathematical scale in the point of the flattening of the fifth. Take for example 1C, and for convenience of figuring, say it vibrates 128 per second. The relation of a fundamental to its fifth is that of 2 to 3. So if 128 is represented as 2, we think of it as 2 times 64. Then with another 64 added, we have 192, which represents 3. In other words, a fundamental has just two-thirds of the number of vibrations per second that its fifth has, in the exact scale. This would mean a fifth in which there would be no beats. Now in the tempered scale we find that G vibrates 191.78 instead of 192; so we can easily see how much variation from the mathematical standard there is in this portion of the instrument. It is only about a fourth of a vibration. This would mean that, in this fifth we would hear the beats a little slower than one per second. Take the same fifth an octave higher and take 2C as fundamental, which has 256 for its vibration number. The G, fifth above, should vibrate 384, but in the tempered scale it beats but 383.57, almost half a vibration flat. This would give nearly 2 beats in 3 seconds.

These figures simply represent to the eye the ratios of these sounds, and it is not supposed that a tuner is to attain to such a degree of accuracy, but he should strive to arrive as near it as possible.

It is well for the student to practice temperament setting and regular tuning now if he can do so.   After getting a good temperament, proceed to tune by octaves upward, always testing the tone tuned as a fifth and third until his ear becomes sufficiently true on the octave that testing otherwise is unnecessary. Tune the overstrung bass last and your work is finished. If your first efforts are at all satisfactory you should be greatly encouraged and feel assured that accuracy will reward continued practice.

QUESTIONS ON LESSON X.

1. What is meant by the term "equal temperament"?

2. What is meant by the term "unequal temperament"?

3. Webster defines the term "temperament" thus: "A system of compromises in the tuning of pianofortes, organs, etc."   Explain fully what these compromises are.

4. In testing chords to ascertain if temperament is correct, what is the main thing to listen for as a guide?

5. In what three chords would you try the tone A, in testing your temperament?

6. With what results have you demonstrated the experiments in this and the previous lesson?

LESSON XI.

THE TECHNIQUE OR MODUS OPERANDI OF PIANO TUNING.

At this juncture, it is thought prudent to defer the discussion of scale building and detail some of the requirements connected with the technical operations of tuning. We do this here because some students are, at this stage, beginning to tune and unless instructed in these things will take hold of the work in an unfavorable way and, perhaps, form habits that will be hard to break. Especially is this so in the matter of setting the mutes or wedges. As to our discussion of scale building, we shall take that up again, that you may be more thoroughly informed on that subject.

Some mechanics do more work in a given time than others, do it as well or better, and with less exertion. This is because they have method or system in their work so that there are no movements lost. Every motion is made to count for the advancement of the cause. Others go about things in a reckless way, taking no thought as to time and labor-saving methods.

In spite of any instruction that can be given, the beginner in piano tuning will not be able to take hold of his work with the ease and the grace of the veteran, nor will he ever be able to work with great accuracy and expedition unless he has a systematic method of doing the various things incident to his profession.

In this lesson, as its subject implies, we endeavor to tell you just how to begin and the way to proceed, step by step, through the work, to obtain the best results in the shortest time, with the greatest ease and the least confusion.

Manipulation of the Tuning Hammer.

It may seem that the tightening of a string by turning a pin, around which it is wound, by the aid of an instrument fitting its square end, is such a simple operation that it should require no skill. Simply tightening a string in this manner is, to be sure, a simple matter; but there is a definite degree of tension at which the *vibrating section* of the string must be left, and it should be left in such a condition that the tension will remain invariable, or as near so as is possible. The only means given the tuner by which he is to bring about this condition are his tuning hammer and the key of the piano, with its mechanism, whereby he may strike the string he is tuning.

The purpose of the tuning hammer is that of altering the tension. The purpose of striking the string by means of the key is twofold: first, to ascertain the pitch of the string, and second, to equalize the tension of the string over its entire length. Consider the string in its three sections, viz.: lower dead end (from hitch pin to lower bridge), vibrating section (section between the bridges), and upper dead end (from upper bridge to tuning pin).

When placing the hammer on the tuning pin and turning to the right, it is evident that the increased tension will be manifest first in the upper dead end. In pianos having agraffes or upper bridges with a tightly screwed bearing bar which makes the strings draw very hard through the bridge, some considerable tension may be produced in the upper dead end before the string will draw through the bridge and increase the tension in the vibrating middle. In other pianos the strings "render" very easily over the upper bridge, and the slightest turn of the hammer manifests an alteration of pitch in the vibrating section. As a rule, strings "render" much more easily through the upper, than the lower bridge. There are two reasons for this: One is, that the construction of the lower bridge is such as to cause a tendency in this direction, having two bridge-pins which stand out of line with the string and bear against it in opposite directions; the other is that the lower bridge is so much farther from the point where the hammer strikes the string that its vibration does not help it through as it does at the upper bridge.

Now, the thing desired is to have the tension equally distributed over the entire length of the string. Tension should be the same in the three different sections. This is of paramount importance. If this condition does not obtain, the piano will not stand in tune. Yet, this is not the only item of importance. The tuning pin must be properly "set," as tuners term it.

By "setting the pins," we mean, leaving it so balanced with respect to the pull of the string that it will neither yield to the pull of the string nor tend to draw it tighter. Coming now to the exact manipulation of the tuning hammer, there are some important items to consider.* Now, if the tuning hammer is placed upon the tuning pin with the handle straight upward, and it is pulled backward (from the tuner) just a little, before it is turned to the right, the tension will be increased somewhat before the pin is turned, as this motion, slight as it may seem, pulls the pin upward enough to draw the string through the upper bridge an infinitesimally small distance, but enough to be perceptible to the ear. Now if the hammer were removed, the tendency of the pin would be to yield to the pull of the string; but if the pin is turned enough to take up such amount of string as was pulled through the bridge, and, as it is turned, is allowed to yield downward toward the pull of the string, it will resume its balance and the string will stand at that pitch, provided it has been "rendered" properly over the bridges.

We set forth these details that you may have a thorough understanding of what is meant by setting the pins, and while it is not always advisable to

* Bear in mind, the foregoing and following instructions are written with reference to the upright piano. The square does not permit the observance of these suggestions so favorably as the upright.

follow this method in tuning, there are some pianos that will stand more satisfactorily when treated in this way. This method is recommended where the string has become rusty at the upper bridge, as it is loosened at the bridge before it is started to wind around the pin which prevents it breaking at that point. We believe that ninety per cent. of strings break right where they start around tuning pin. A very good way to draw a string up is to give the hammer an alternate up and down motion, pulling the handle lightly to you, then from you, as you draw it up; not enough to bend or break the pin or to crush the wood around the pin, but just enough to make the string take on its increased tension equally.

In regard to the lower bridge, the strings will rarely "render" through them properly unless brought to a tension a little higher than it is desired they shall be left. If this is done, a few sharp blows of key will generally make them equalize all right; then press the hammer gently to the left, not enough to turn the pin in the socket, but to settle it back to a well-balanced position. After a little practice the tuner can generally guess precisely how much

over-tension to allow. If the pin is left slightly
sprung downward, its tendency will be to spring upward, thereby sharpening the string; so be careful
to leave the pins in perfect balance, or as tuners say,
"properly set."

The foregoing, while applicable to the whole scale,
is not so urgent in the over-strung bass. The strings
are so heavy and the tension is so great that they
will generally "render" quite freely over the bridges,
and it is only necessary to bring them up to pitch,
handling the hammer in such a manner as to leave
the pins well balanced; but it is not necessary to
give them over-tension and beat them down again;
in fact it is not advisable, as a rule. At all times,
place the hammer on the pin as far as it will go, and
strike the key while drawing a string up.

In tuning the square piano, it is not possible to
set the hammer upon the pin with the handle in line
with, and beyond the string, as is the rule in the upright. Where the square has the square pin, the
hammer (with star head) can always be set with the
handle to the right of the string somewhat, but
usually almost in line with the string and almost
directly over it, and the manipulation of the hammer

is much the same, though the tuner is at a greater disadvantage, the pins being farther from him and he has not such a good rest for his hand. Many old squares have the oblong pin. In this case, use the double hammer head. On the one side the hole in the head is made with the longer diameter in line with the handle, and on the other side the hole is made with the longer diameter at right angles with the handle; so that if you cannot get a favorable position with one end you can with the other.

We have said nothing about which hand to use in striking the keys and in wielding the hammer, but it is customary to handle the hammer with the right hand and it is always advisable for two very good reasons: It gives the tuner a much more favorable position at the instrument; and, as the right hand is more used in ordinary every-day operations and is more trained in applying degrees of force and guiding tools, it is more easily trained to manipulate the hammer properly. Training the hand in the skilful use of the hammer is of the utmost importance and comes only by continued practice, but when it is trained, one can virtually "feel" the tones with the hammer.

At first, the young tuner is almost invariably discouraged by his slow progress. He must remember that, however fine his ear and however great his mechanical ability, he has much to acquire by training in both, and he must expect to be two or three times longer in finishing off a job of tuning at the outset than will be necessary after he has had a few months' practice. You can be your own trainer in these things if you will do a little rational thinking and be content to "hasten slowly." And as to using the left hand, we would not advise it in any event.

Setting the Mutes or Wedges in the Upright.

As stated in a previous lesson, the mutes should be so placed that only two strings are heard at one time: the one the tuner is tuning, and the one he is tuning by. It is true that this is an easy matter, but it is also true that very few tuners know how to do it in a way to save time and avoid placing the mutes two or more times in the same place. By using a little inventive genius during early practice the author succeeded in formulating a system of muting by which he accomplished the ends as stated above, and assures the reader that a great deal of time can be saved by following it.

After removing the muffler or any other instrumental attachment which may be in the piano in the way of placing the mutes, the first thing to do is to place the continuous mute so thåt all the outside strings of the trios are damped. The temperament is then set by tuning the middle strings, of the twenty-five trios comprised in the two-octave temperament as demonstrated in a previous lesson. After satisfying yourself by trials or test that the temperament is true, you then remove the continuous mute and proceed to bring the outside strings in unison with the middle one. Now, your 1C is sometimes found to be the first pair in the over-strung bass, which usually has two strings to a key, while in other pianos, 1C is the first trio in the treble stringing, ånd in many cases it is the second trio in the treble. For illustration, we will say it is the second in the treble. In speaking of the separate strings of a trio we will number them 1st, 2d, and 3d, from left to right, as in foot-note, page 89, Lesson IX. Setting the mutes in bringing up the unisons in the temperament is exceedingly simple.

The following diagram will, we think, demonstrate clearly the method employed:

```
Upper row ----   o  o  o  o  o  o  o  o  o  o      Tun-
Middle row ---   o  o  o  o  o  o  o  o  o  o      ing
Lower row ---    o  o  o  o  o  o  o  o  o  o      Pins.
─────────────────────────────────────────────    Bridge.
        /#/ 1/#/ 2/#/ 3/#/ 4/#/ 5/#/ 6/#/ 7/#/ 8/#/ 9/#/  &c  Treble Stringing
        B   C   C#  D   D#  E   F   F#  G   G#   &c
```

The upper row of o's represents the upper row of tuning pins. To these are attached the first string of each unison. To the middle row are attached the second or middle strings, and to the lower row are attached the third strings. The diagonal lines represent the three strings of the unison (trio). The asterisk on the middle one indicates that it has been tuned.

But one mute is used in tuning these unisons. It is inserted between the trios in the order indicated by the figures 1, 2, 3, etc. When inserted in place 1, between unisons B and C, it will mute the first string of C; so the first string of the trio to tune is always the third. Then place your mute in place 2 and tune the first string of C. Then, without moving your mute, bring up third string of C♯, then third string of D and so on. By this method, you tune two strings every time you reset your mute.

When through with the temperament, the next step is usually that of tuning the bass; but while we are in the treble we will proceed to give the method of setting the mutes in the upper treble beyond the temperament. All three strings have yet to be tuned here, and we have to use two mutes. The unisons are tuned in regular succession upward the same as in the example above. The mute that is kept farthest to the left, is indicated by the letter A, and the one kept to the right, by the letter B, as in diagram below.

The mutes are first placed in the places indicated by the figures 1 and 2, thereby muting first and third strings of the first unison beyond the temperament, which is 3C♯. The middle string of this unison is now tuned by its octave below. (If you have left imperfect unisons in your temperament, rendering it difficult to tune octaves by them, it will be well to replace your continuous mute so as to tune from a single string.)   Having tuned the middle string of C♯, move mute B to place 3 and tune third string of C♯.   Then, move mute A to place 2 and tune first string of C♯ .   Your mutes are now already set for tuning the middle string of D.   After this is done, proceed to move mute B first, then mute A; tuning middle string, then third, then first, moving step by step as indicated in example above until the last unison is reached.   By this system you tune three strings every time the mutes are set twice.

The over-strung bass usually has but two strings to a unison and only one mute is needed.   In the extreme low or contra-bass, pianos have but one string, in tuning which the mute is discarded.   Set the mute as indicated by the figures 1, 2, 3, etc., in the diagram below, always tuning the string farthest to the right by its octave above; then move the mute to its next place and tune the left string by the right.   Here, again, you tune two strings every time you reset your mute.   The I's represent bass strings.

```
                          9   8   7   6   5   4   3   2   1
I   I   I   I   I   I   I   II  II  II  II  II  II  II  II  II
                 C  C♯  D  D♯  E   F   F♯  G  G♯  A  A♯   B  C
    Contra-Bass.                 Bass.                  Treble.
```

SETTING THE MUTES IN THE SQUARE PIANO.

In setting the temperament in the square piano, simply mute the string farthest to the left and tune the one to the right until the temperament is finished, then set the mutes in the bass the same as in the upright. In tuning the treble, if the piano has three strings, the same system is used as has been described for the upright. When the piano has but two strings to a unison, as is usually the case, employ the system described for the bass of the upright, but reversed, as you are proceeding to the right instead of to the left.

Remove the shade before beginning to tune a square piano, and if necessary, lay the dampers back and trace the strings to their pins so as to mark them. Certain pins are marked to guide the tuner in placing his hammer. The way we have always marked them is as follows:

Mark both pins of each pair of C strings with white crayon. Mark only one pin of each pair of G's. Knowing the intervals of the other keys from the marked ones, you can easily calculate correctly, upon which pin to set your hammer to tune any string desired. For instance, if you are striking D♯, next above middle C, you calculate that, as D♯ is the third chromatic interval from middle C, you are to set the hammer on one or the other of the pins belonging to the third pair to the right of the pair marked as middle C. B would be first pair to the left, F♯ would be first pair to the left of the marked G, and so on. It is usually necessary to mark only those pairs near the middle of the piano, but we advise the beginner to mark throughout the scale, as by so doing he may avoid breaking a string occasionally by pulling on some other than the one he is sounding. This will occur in your early practice if you do not use caution. And for safety, some tuners always mark throughout.

QUESTIONS ON LESSON XI.

1. By what means is the tuner enabled to make the strings draw through the bridges and equalize the tension throughout their entire length?
2. State conditions that may result from a tuning pin's not being properly set.

3. In this system of muting, state definitely which string is tuned first after the continuous mute is removed. Which second? Which third?

4. After the unisons are finished in the temperament, which string is tuned next, if we go immediately from the temperament to the over-strung bass? Which second? Which third?

5. Upon beginning to tune the treble beyond the temperament, which string is tuned first? Which second? Which third?

6. (a) How many mutes are used in tuning outside the strings of the temperament?

   (b) In what proportion is the number of times the mute is changed to the number of strings tuned?

7. (a) How many mutes are used in tuning the treble beyond the temperament?

   (b) In what proportion is the number of times the mute is changed to the number of strings tuned?

8. Which pairs of pins are marked in the square piano to guide the tuner in placing his hammer? Also, how are they marked?

9. Having marked your pins as instructed, how would you find the pins belonging to a pair of strings struck by F on key-board? How those struck by G#?

10. Tell what you can of the requirements necessary to insure that a piano will stand in tune.

LESSON XII.

MATHEMATICS OF THE TEMPERED SCALE.

One of the first questions that arises in the mind of the thinking young tuner is: Why is it necessary to temper certain intervals in tuning? We cannot answer this question in a few words; but you have seen, if you have tried the experiments laid down in previous lessons, that such deviation is inevitable. You know that practical scale making will permit but two pure intervals (unison and octave), but you have yet to learn the scientific reasons why this is so. To do this, requires a little mathematical reasoning.

In this lesson we shall demonstrate the principles of this complex subject in a clear and comprehensive way, and if you will study it carefully you may master it thoroughly, which will place you in possession of a knowledge of the art of which few tuners of the present can boast.

In the following demonstrations of relative pitch numbers, we adopt a pitch in which middle C has 256 vibrations per second. This is not a pitch which is used in actual practice, as it is even below international (middle C 258.65); but is chosen on account of the fact that the various relative pitch numbers work out more favorably, and hence, it is called the "Philosophical Standard." Below are the actual vibration numbers of the two pitches in vogue; so you can see that neither of these pitches would be so favorable to deal with mathematically.

International—3C–517.3.   Concert—3C–540.

(Let us state here that the difference in these pitches is less than a half-step, but is so near that it is generally spoken of as being just a half-step.)

Temperament denotes the arrangement of a system of musical sounds in which *each one* will form a serviceable interval with *any one* of the others. Any given tone must do duty as the initial or key-note of a major or of a minor scale and also as any other member; thus:

C must serve as 1, in the key of C major or C minor.
"   "   2,   "   " B♭   "   B♭   "
"   "   3,   "   " A♭   "   A   "
"   "   4,   "   " G   "   G   "
"   "   5,   "   " F   "   F   "
"   "   6,   "   " E♭   "   E   "
"   "   7,   "   " D♭   "   C♯   "

Likewise, all other tones of the instrument must be so stationed that they can serve as *any member* of *any scale*, major or minor.

This is rendered necessary on account of the various modulations employed in modern music, in which every possible harmony in every key is used.

RATIONALE OF THE TEMPERAMENT.

Writers upon the mathematics of sound tell us, experience teaches us, and in previous lessons we have demonstrated in various ways, that if we tune all fifths perfect up to the seventh step (see diagram, pages 82, 83) the last E obtained will be too sharp to form a major third to C. In fact, the third thus obtained is so sharp as to render it offensive to the ear, and therefore unfit for use in harmony, where this interval plays so conspicuous a part. To remedy this, it becomes necessary to tune each of the fifths a very small degree flatter than perfect. The E thus obtained will not be so sharp as to be offensive to the ear; yet, if the fifth be properly altered or tempered, the third will still be sharper than perfect; for if the fifths were flattened enough to render the thirds perfect, they (the fifths) would become offensive. Now, it is a fact, that the third will bear greater deviation from perfect consonance than the fifth; so the compromise is made somewhat in favor of the fifth. If we should continue the series of perfect fifths, we will find the same defect in all the major thirds throughout the scale.

We must, therefore, flatten each fifth of the complete circle, C–G–D–A–E–B–F♯–C♯–G♯ or A♭–E♭–B♭–F–C, successively in a very small degree; the depression, while it will not materially impair the consonant quality of the fifths, will produce a series of somewhat sharp, though still agreeable and harmonious major thirds.

We wish, now, to demonstrate the cause of the foregoing by mathematical calculation, which, while it is somewhat lengthy and tedious, is not difficult if followed progressively. First, we will consider tone relationship in connection with relative string length. Students who have small stringed instruments, guitar, violin, or mandolin, may find pleasure in demonstrating some of the following facts thereupon.

One-half of any string will produce a tone exactly an octave above that yielded by its entire length. Harmonic tones on the violin are made by

touching the string lightly with the finger at such
points as will cause the string to vibrate in segments;
thus if touched exactly in the middle it will produce
a harmonic tone an octave above that of the whole
string.

Two-thirds of the length of a string when stopped
produces a tone a fifth higher than that of the entire
string; one-third of the length of a string on the
violin, either from the nut or from the bridge, if
touched lightly with the finger at that point, produces
a harmonic tone an octave higher than the fifth to
the open tone of that string, because you divide the
string into three vibrating segments, each of which
is one-third its entire length.   Reason it thus: If two-
thirds of a string produce a fifth, one-third, being just
half of two-thirds, will produce a tone an octave higher
than two-thirds.   For illustration, if the string be
tuned to 1C, the harmonic tone produced as above
will be 2G.   We might go on for pages concerning
harmonics, but for our present use it is only necessary to show the general principles.   For our needs
we will discuss the relative length of string necessary to produce the various tones of the diatonic
scale, showing ratios of the intervals in the same.

In the following table, I represents the entire length of a string sounding the tone C. The other tones of the ascending major scale require strings of such fractional length as are indicated by the fractions beneath them. By taking accurate measurements you can demonstrate these figures upon any small stringed instrument.

FUNDA-MENTAL	MAJOR SECOND	MAJOR THIRD	PERFECT FOURTH	PERFECT FIFTH	MAJOR SIXTH	MAJOR SEVENTH	OCTAVE
C	D	E	F	G	A	B	C
I	$\frac{8}{9}$	$\frac{4}{5}$	$\frac{3}{4}$	$\frac{2}{3}$	$\frac{3}{5}$	$\frac{8}{15}$	$\frac{1}{2}$

To illustrate this principle further and make it very clear, let us suppose that the entire length of the string sounding the fundamental C is 360 inches; then the segments of this string necessary to produce the other tones of the ascending major scale will be, in inches, as follows:

C	D	E	F	G	A	B	C
360	320	288	270	240	216	192	180

Comparing now one with another (by means of the ratios expressed by their corresponding numbers) the intervals formed by the tones of the above scale, it will be found that they all preserve their original purity except the minor third, D–F, and the fifth, D–A. The third, D–F, presents itself in the ratio of 320 to 270 instead of 324 to 270 (which latter is equivalent to the ratio of 6 to 5, the true ratio of the minor third). The third, D–F, therefore, is to the true minor third as 320 to 324 (reduced to their lowest terms by dividing both numbers by 4, gives the ratio of 80 to 81). Again, the fifth, A–F, presents itself in the ratio of 320 to 216, or (dividing each term by 4) 80 to 54; instead of 3 to 2 (= 81 to 54— multiplying each term by 27), which is the ratio of the true fifth. Continuing the scale an octave higher, it will be found that the sixth, F–D, and the fourth, A–D, will labor under the same imperfections.

The comparison, then, of these ratios of the minor third, D–F, and the fifth, D–A, with the perfect ratios of these intervals, shows that each is too small by the ratio expressed by the figures 80 to 81. This is called, by mathematicians, the *syntonic comma*.

As experience teaches us that the ear cannot endure such deviation as a whole comma in any fifth, it is easy to see that some tempering must take place even in such a simple and limited number of sounds as the above series of eight tones.

The necessity of temperament becomes still more apparent when it is proposed to combine every sound used in music into a connected system, such that each individual sound shall not only form practical intervals with all the other sounds, but also that each sound may be employed as the root of its own major or minor key; and that all the tones necessary to form its scale shall stand in such relation to each other as to satisfy the ear.

The chief requisites of any system of musical temperament adapted to the purposes of modern music are:—

1. That all octaves must remain perfect, each being divided into twelve semitones.

2. That each sound of the system may be employed as the root of a major or minor scale, without increasing the number of sounds in the system.

3. That each consonant interval, according to its degree of consonance, shall lose as little of its original purity as possible; so that the ear may still acknowledge it as a perfect or imperfect consonance.

Several ways of adjusting such a system of temperament have been proposed, all of which may be classed under either the head of equal or of unequal temperament.

The principles set forth in the following propositions clearly demonstrate the reasons for tempering, and the whole rationale of the system of equal temperament, which is that in general use, and which is invariably sought and practiced by tuners of the present.

PROPOSITION I.

If we divide an octave, as from middle C to 3C, into three major thirds, each in the perfect ratio of 5 to 4, as C–E, E–G♯ (A♭), A♭–C, then the C obtained from the last third, A♭–C, will be too flat to form a perfect octave by a small quantity, called in the theory of harmonics a *diesis*, which is expressed by the ratio 128 to 125.

EXPLANATION.—The length of the string sounding the tone C is represented by unity or I. Now, as we have shown, the major third to that C, which is E, is produced by $\frac{4}{5}$ of its length.

In like manner, G♯, the major third to E, will be produced by $\frac{4}{5}$ of that segment of the string which sounds the tone E; that is, G♯ will be produced by $\frac{4}{5}$ of $\frac{4}{5}$ ($\frac{4}{5}$ multiplied by $\frac{4}{5}$) which equals $\frac{16}{25}$ of the entire length of the string sounding the tone C.

We come, now, to the last third, G♯ (A♭) to C, which completes the interval of the octave, middle C to 3C. This last C, being the major third from the A♭, will be produced as before, by $\frac{4}{5}$ of that segment of the string which sounds A♭; that is, by $\frac{4}{5}$ of $\frac{16}{25}$, which equals $\frac{64}{125}$ of the entire length of the string. Keep this last fraction, $\frac{64}{125}$, in mind, and remember it as representing the segment of the entire string, which produces the upper C by the succession of three perfectly tuned major thirds.

Now, let us refer to the law which says that a perfect octave is obtained from the exact half of the length of any string. Is $\frac{64}{125}$ an exact half? No; using the same numerator, an exact half would be $\frac{64}{128}$.

Hence, it is clear that the octave obtained by the succession of perfect major thirds will differ from the true octave by the ratio of 128 to 125. The fraction, $\frac{64}{125}$, representing a longer segment of the string than $\frac{64}{128}$ ($\frac{1}{2}$), it would produce a flatter tone than the exact half.

It is evident, therefore, that *all major thirds must be tuned somewhat sharper than perfect* in a system of equal temperament.

The ratio which expresses the value of the *diesis* is that of 128 to 125. If, therefore, the octaves are to remain perfect, which they must do, *each major third must be tuned sharper than perfect by one-third part of the diesis.*

The foregoing demonstration may be made still clearer by the following diagram which represents the length of string necessary to produce these tones. (This diagram is exact in the various proportional lengths, being about one twenty-fifth the actual length represented.)

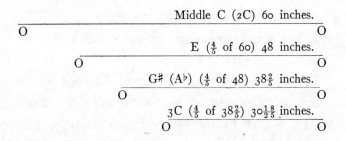

Middle C (2C) 60 inches.

E ($\frac{4}{5}$ of 60) 48 inches.

G♯ (A♭) ($\frac{4}{5}$ of 48) 38$\frac{2}{5}$ inches.

3C ($\frac{4}{5}$ of 38$\frac{2}{5}$) 30$\frac{18}{25}$ inches.

This diagram clearly demonstrates that the last C obtained by the succession of thirds covers a segment of the string which is $\frac{18}{25}$ longer than an exact half; nearly three-fourths of an inch too long, 30 inches being the exact half.

To make this proposition still better understood, we give the comparison of the actual vibration numbers as follows:—

Perfect thirds in ratio $\frac{4}{5}$ have these vibration numbers: $=$	1st third (C 256–E 320) no beats	2d third (E 320–G♯ 400) no beats	3d third (G♯ 400–C 500) no beats
Tempered thirds qualified to produce true octave: $=$	(C 256–E $322\frac{5}{10}$) 10 beats	(E $322\frac{5}{10}$–G♯ $406\frac{4}{10}$) $13\frac{1}{10}$ beats	(G♯ $406\frac{4}{10}$–C 512) 16 beats

We think the foregoing elucidation of Proposition I sufficient to establish a thorough understanding of the facts set forth therein, if they are studied over carefully a few times. If everything is not clear at the first reading, go over it several times, as this matter is of value to you.

QUESTIONS ON LESSON XII.

1. Why is the pitch, C–256, adopted for scientific discussion, and what is this pitch called?

2. The tone G forms the root (1) in the key of G. What does it form in the key of C? What in F? What in D?

3. What tone is produced by a ⅔ segment of a string?
   What by a ½ segment? What by a ⅘ segment?

4. (a) What intervals must be tuned absolutely
       perfect?

   (b) In the two intervals that must be tempered,
       the third and the fifth, which will bear the
       greater deviation?

5. What would be the result if we should tune from
   2C to 3C by a succession of perfect thirds?

6. Do you understand the facts set forth in Proposition I, in this lesson?

LESSON XIII.

RATIONALE OF THE TEMPERAMENT.
(Concluded from Lesson XII.)

PROPOSITION II.

That the student of scientific scale building may understand fully the reasons why the tempered scale is at constant variance with exact mathematical ratios, we continue this discussion through two more propositions, No. II, following, demonstrating the result of dividing the octave into four minor thirds, and Proposition III, demonstrating the result of twelve perfect fifths. The matter in Lesson XII, if properly mastered, has given a thorough insight into the principal features of the subject in question; so the following demonstration will be made as brief as possible, consistent with clearness.

Let us figure the result of dividing an octave into four minor thirds. The ratio of the length of string sounding a fundamental, to the length necessary to sound its minor third, is that of 6 to 5. In other words, $\frac{5}{6}$ of any string sounds a tone which is an exact minor third above that of the whole string.

Now, suppose we select, as before, a string sounding middle C, as the fundamental tone. We now ascend by minor thirds until we reach the C, octave above middle C, which we call 3C, as follows:

Middle C–E♭; E♭–F♯; F♯–A; A–3C.

Demonstrate by figures as follows:—Let the whole length of string sounding middle C be represented by unity or 1.

E♭ will be sounded by $\frac{5}{6}$ of the string .... $\frac{5}{6}$

F♯, by $\frac{5}{6}$ of the E♭ segment; that is, by $\frac{5}{6}$ of $\frac{5}{6}$ of the entire string, which equals .... $\frac{25}{36}$

A, by $\frac{5}{6}$ of $\frac{25}{36}$ of entire string, which equals .... $\frac{125}{216}$

3C, by $\frac{5}{6}$ of $\frac{125}{216}$ of entire string, which equals .... $\frac{625}{1296}$

Now bear in mind, this last fraction, $\frac{625}{1296}$, represents the segment of the entire string which should sound the tone 3C, an exact octave above middle C. Remember, our law demands an exact half of a string by which to sound its octave. How much does it vary? Divide the denominator (1296) by 2 and place the result over it for a numerator, and this gives $\frac{648}{1296}$, which is an exact half. Notice the comparison.

3C obtained from a succession of exact minor thirds, $\frac{625}{1296}$
3C obtained from an exact half of the string ...... $\frac{648}{1296}$

Now, the former fraction is smaller than the latter; hence, the segment of string which it represents will be shorter than the exact half, and will consequently yield a sharper tone. The denominators being the same, we have only to find the difference between the numerators to tell how much too short the former segment is. This proves the C obtained by the succession of minor thirds to be too short by $\frac{23}{1296}$ of the length of the whole string.

If, therefore, all octaves are to remain perfect, it is evident that *all minor thirds must be tuned flatter than perfect* in the system of equal temperament.

The ratio, then, of 648 to 625 expresses the excess by which the true octave exceeds four exact minor thirds; consequently, each minor third must be flatter than perfect by one-fourth part of the difference between these fractions. By this means the dissonance is evenly distributed so that it is not noticeable in the various chords, in the major and minor keys, where this interval is almost invariably present. (We find no record of writers on the mathematics of sound giving a name to the above ratio expressing variance, as they have to others.)

PROPOSITION III.

Proposition III deals with the perfect fifth, showing the result from a series of twelve perfect fifths employed within the space of an octave.

METHOD.—Taking 1C as the fundamental, representing it by unity or 1, the G, fifth above, is sounded by a $\frac{2}{3}$ segment of the string sounding C. The next fifth, G–D, takes us beyond the octave, and we find that the D will be sounded by $\frac{4}{9}$ ($\frac{2}{3}$ of $\frac{2}{3}$ equals $\frac{4}{9}$) of the entire string, which fraction is less than half; so to keep within the bounds of the octave, we must double this segment and make it sound the tone D an octave lower, thus: $\frac{4}{9}$ times 2 equals $\frac{8}{9}$, the segment sounding the D within the octave.

We may shorten the operation as follows: Instead of multiplying $\frac{2}{3}$ by $\frac{2}{3}$, giving us $\frac{4}{9}$, and then multiplying this answer by 2, let us double the fraction, $\frac{2}{3}$, which equals $\frac{4}{3}$, and use it as a multiplier when it becomes necessary to double the segment to keep within the octave.

We may proceed now with the twelve steps as follows:—

Steps—

1. 1C to 1G....................segment $\frac{2}{3}$ for 1G
2. 1G " 1D Multiply $\frac{2}{3}$ by $\frac{4}{3}$, gives segment $\frac{8}{9}$ " 1D
3. 1D " 1A " $\frac{8}{9}$ " $\frac{2}{3}$ " " $\frac{16}{27}$ " 1A
4. 1A " 1E " $\frac{16}{27}$ " $\frac{4}{3}$ " " $\frac{64}{81}$ " 1E
5. 1E " 1B " $\frac{64}{81}$ " $\frac{2}{3}$ " " $\frac{128}{243}$ " 1B
6. 1B " 1F# " $\frac{128}{243}$ " $\frac{4}{3}$ " " $\frac{512}{729}$ " 1F#
7. 1F# " 1C# " $\frac{512}{729}$ " $\frac{4}{3}$ " " $\frac{2048}{2187}$ " 1C#
8. 1C# " 1G# " $\frac{2048}{2187}$ " $\frac{2}{3}$ " " $\frac{4096}{6561}$ " 1G#
9. 1G# " 1D# " $\frac{4096}{6561}$ " $\frac{4}{3}$ " " $\frac{16384}{19683}$ " 1D#
10. 1D# " 1A# " $\frac{16384}{19683}$ " $\frac{2}{3}$ " " $\frac{32768}{59049}$ " 1A#
11. 1A# " 1F " $\frac{32768}{59049}$ " $\frac{4}{3}$ " " $\frac{131072}{177147}$ " 1F
12. 1F " 2C " $\frac{131072}{177147}$ " $\frac{2}{3}$ " " $\frac{262144}{531441}$ " 2C

Now, this last fraction should be equivalent to $\frac{1}{2}$, when reduced to its lowest terms, if it is destined to produce a true octave; but, using this numerator, 262144, a half would be expressed by $\frac{262144}{524288}$, the segment producing the true octave; so the fraction $\frac{262144}{531441}$, which represents the segment for 2C, obtained by the circle of fifths, being evidently less than $\frac{1}{2}$, this segment will yield a tone somewhat sharper than the true octave. The two denominators are taken in this case to show the ratio of the variance; so the octave obtained from the circle of fifths is sharper than the true octave in the ratio expressed by 531441 to 524288, which ratio is called the *ditonic comma*. This comma is equal to one-fifth of a half-step.

We are to conclude, then, that if octaves are to remain perfect, and we desire to establish an equal temperament, the above-named difference is best disposed of by dividing it into twelve equal parts and depressing each of the fifths one-twelfth part of the ditonic comma; thereby dispersing the dissonance so that it will allow perfect octaves, and yet, but slightly impair the consonance of the fifths.

We believe the foregoing propositions will demonstrate the facts stated therein, to the student's satisfaction, and that he should now have a pretty thorough knowledge of the mathematics of the temperament. That the equal temperament is the only practical temperament, is confidently affirmed by Mr. W. S. B. Woolhouse, an eminent authority on musical mathematics, who says:—

"It is very misleading to suppose that the necessity of temperament applies only to instruments which have fixed tones. Singers and performers on perfect instruments must all temper their intervals, or they could not keep in tune with each other, or even with themselves; and on arriving at the same notes by different routes, would be continually finding a want of agreement. The scale of equal temperament obviates all such inconveniences, and continues to be universally accepted with unqualified satisfaction by the most eminent vocalists; and equally so by the most renowned and accomplished performers on stringed instruments, although these instruments are capable of an indefinite variety of intonation. The high development of modern instrumental music would not have been possible, and could not have been acquired, without the manifold advantages of the tempered intonation by equal semitones, and it has, in consequence, long become the established basis of tuning."

NUMERICAL COMPARISON OF THE DIATONIC SCALE WITH THE TEMPERED SCALE.

The following table, comparing vibration numbers of the diatonic scale with those of the tempered, shows the difference in the two scales, existing between the thirds, fifths and other intervals.

Notice that the difference is but slight in the lowest octave used which is shown on the left; but taking the scale four octaves higher, shown on the right, the difference becomes more striking.

DIATONIC.		TEMPERED.	DIATONIC.		TEMPERED.
C	32.	........32.	C	512.	.... 512.
D	36.	........35.92	D	576.	.... 574.70
E	40.	........40.32	E	640.	.... 645.08
F	42.66	........42.71	F	682.66	.... 683.44
G	48.	........47.95	G	768.	.... 767.13
A	53.33	........53.82	A	853.33	.... 861.08
B	60.	........60.41	B	960.	.... 966.53
C	64.	........64.	C	1024.	.......1024.

Following this paragraph we give a reference table in which the numbers are given for four consecutive octaves, calculated for the system of equal temperament. Each column represents an octave. The first two columns cover the tones of the two octaves used in setting the temperament by our system.

TABLE OF VIBRATIONS PER SECOND.

C........128.	256.	512.	1024.
C# 135.61	271.22	542.44	1084.89
D 143.68	287.35	574.70	1149.40
D# 152.22	304.44	608.87	1217.75
E........161.27	322.54	645.08	1290.16
F........170.86	341.72	683.44	1366.87

TABLE OF VIBRATIONS PER SECOND (Continued).

F♯	. . . . . . .181.02	362.04	724.08	1448.15
G	. . . . . . .191.78	383.57	767.13	1534.27
G♯	. . . . . .203.19	406.37	812.75	1625.50
A	. . . . .215.27	430.54	861.08	1722.16
A♯	. . . . . . .228.07	456.14	912.28	1824.56
B	. . . . . . .241.63	483.26	966.53	1933.06
C	. . . . . . .256.	512.	1024.	2048.

Much interesting and valuable exercise may be derived from the investigation of this table by figuring out what certain intervals would be if exact, and then comparing them with the figures shown in this tempered scale. To do this, select two notes and ascertain what interval the higher forms to the lower; then, by the fraction in the table below corresponding to that interval, multiply the vibration number of the lower note.

EXAMPLE.—Say we select the first C, 128, and the G in the same column. We know this to be an interval of a perfect fifth. Referring to the table below, we find that the vibration of the fifth is $\frac{3}{2}$ of, or $\frac{3}{2}$ times, that of its fundamental; so we simply multiply this fraction by the vibration number of C, which is 128, and this gives 192 as the exact fifth.

Now, on referring to the above table of equal temperament, we find this G quoted a little less (flatter), viz., 191.78. To find a fourth from any note, multiply its number by $\frac{4}{3}$, a major third, by $\frac{5}{4}$, and so on as per table below.

TABLE SHOWING RELATIVE VIBRATION OF INTERVALS BY IMPROPER FRACTIONS.

The relation of the Octave to a Fundamental is expressed by.....$\frac{2}{1}$

"	"	" Fifth to a	"	"	.........$\frac{3}{2}$
"	"	" Fourth to a	"	"	...........$\frac{4}{3}$
"	"	" Major Third to a	"	"	.....$\frac{5}{4}$
"	"	" Minor Third to a	"	"	.........$\frac{6}{5}$
"	"	" Major Second to a	"	"	.........$\frac{9}{8}$
"	"	" Major Sixth to a	"	"	.....$\frac{5}{3}$
"	'	" Minor Sixth to a	"	"	.........$\frac{8}{5}$
"	"	" Major Seventh to a	"	"	...........$\frac{15}{8}$
"	"	" Minor Second to a	"	"	....$\frac{16}{15}$

QUESTIONS ON LESSON XIII.

1. State what principle is demonstrated in Proposition II.

2. State what principle is demonstrated in Proposition III.

3. What would be the vibration per second of an exact (not tempered) fifth, from C–512?

4. Give the figures and the process used in finding the vibration number of the *exact* major third to C–256.

5. If we should tune the whole circle of twelve fifths exactly as detailed in Proposition III, how much too sharp would the last C be to the first C tuned?

LESSON XIV.

MISCELLANEOUS TOPICS PERTAINING TO THE PRACTICAL WORK OF TUNING.

Beats.—The phenomenon known as "beats" has been but briefly alluded to in previous lessons, and not analytically discussed as it should be, being so important a feature as it is, in the practical operations of tuning. The average tuner hears and considers the beats with a vague and indefinite comprehension, guessing at causes and effects, and arriving at uncertain results. Having now become familiar with vibration numbers and ratios, the student may, at this juncture, more readily understand the phenomenon, the more scientific discussion of which it has been thought prudent to withhold until now.

In speaking of the unison in Lesson VIII, we stated that "the cause of the waves in a defective unison is the alternate recurring of the periods when the condensations and the rarefactions correspond in the two strings, and then antagonize." This concise definition is complete; but it may not as yet have been fully apprehended. The unison being the simplest interval, we shall use it for consideration before taking the more complex intervals into account.

Let us consider the nature of a single musical tone: that it consists of a chain of sound-waves; that each sound-wave consists of a condensation and a rarefaction, which are directly opposed to each other; and that sound-waves travel through air at a specific rate per second. Let us also remark, here, that in the foregoing lessons, where reference is made to vibrations, the term signifies sound-waves. In other words, the terms, "vibration" and "sound-wave," are synonymous.

If two strings, tuned to give forth the same number of vibrations per second, are struck at the same time, the tone produced will appear to come from a single source; one sweet, continuous, smooth, musical tone. The reason is this: The condensations sent forth from each of the two strings occur exactly together; the rarefactions, which, of course, alternate with the condensations, are also simultaneous.

It necessarily follows, therefore, that the condensations from each of the two strings travel with the same velocity. Now, while this condition prevails, it is evident that the two strings assist each other, making the condensations more condensed, and, consequently, the rarefactions more rarefied, the result of which is, the two allied forces combine to strengthen the tone.

In opposition to the above, if two strings, tuned to produce the same tone, could be so struck that the condensation of one would occur at the same instant with the rarefaction of the other, it is readily seen that the two forces would oppose, or counteract each other, which, if equal, would result in absolute silence.*

* When the bushing of the center-pin of the hammer butt becomes badly worn or the hammer-flange becomes loose, or the condition of the hammer or flange becomes so impaired that the hammer has too much play, it may so strike the strings as to tend to produce the phenomenon described in the above paragraph. When in such a condition, one side of the hammer may strike in advance of the other just enough to throw the vibrations in opposition. Once you may get a strong tone, and again you strike with the same force and hear but a faint, almost inaudible sound. For this reason, as well as that of preventing excessive wear, the hammer joint should be kept firm and rigid.

If one of the strings vibrates 100 times in a second, and the other 101, there will be a portion of time during each second when the vibrations will coincide, and likewise a portion of time when they will antagonize each other. The periods of coincidence and of antagonism pass by progressive transition from one to the other, and the portion of time when exactitude is attained is infinitesimal; so there will be two opposite effects noticed in every second of time: the one, a progressive augmentation of strength and volume, the other, a gradual diminution of the same; the former occurring when the vibrations are coming into coincidence, the latter, when they are approaching the point of antagonism. Therefore, when we speak of one beat per second, we mean that there will be one period of augmentation and one period of diminution in one second. Young tuners sometimes get confused and accept one beat as being two, taking the period of augmentation for one beat and likewise the period of diminution. This is most likely to occur in the lower fifths of the temperament where the beats are very slow.

Two strings struck at the same time, one tuned an octave higher than the other, will vibrate in the ratio of 2 to 1. If these two strings vary from this ratio to the amount of *one* vibration, they will produce *two* beats. Two strings sounding an interval of the fifth vibrate in the ratio of 3 to 2. If they vary from this ratio to the amount of *one* vibration, there will occur *three* beats per second. In the case of the major third, there will occur *four* beats per second to a variation of *one* vibration from the true ratio of 5 to 4. You should bear this in mind in considering the proper number of beats for an interval, the vibration number being known.

It will be seen, from the above facts in connection with the study of the table of vibration numbers in Lesson XIII, that all fifths do not beat alike. The lower the vibration number, the slower the beats. If, at a certain point, a fifth beats once per second, the fifth taken an octave higher will beat twice; and the intervening fifths will beat from a little more than once, up to nearly twice per second, as they approach the higher fifth. Vibrations per second double with each octave, and so do beats.

By referring to the table in Lesson XIII, above referred to, the exact beating of any fifth may be ascertained as follows:—

Ascertain what the vibration number of the *exact* fifth would be, according to the instructions given beneath the table; find the difference between this and the *tempered* fifth given in the table. Multiply this difference by 3, and the result will be the number of beats or fraction thereof, of the tempered fifth. The reason we multiply by 3 is because, as above stated, a variation of one vibration per second in the fifth causes three beats per second.

Example.—Take the first fifth in the table, C–128 to G–191.78, and by the proper calculation (see example, page 147, Lesson XIII) we find the exact fifth to this C would be 192. The difference, then, found by subtracting the smaller from the greater, is .22 ($\frac{22}{100}$). Multiply .22 by 3 and the result is .66, or about two-thirds of a beat per second.

By these calculations we learn that the fifth, C–256 to G–383.57, should have 1.29 beats: nearly one and a third per second, and that the highest fifth of the temperament, F–341.72 to C–512, should be 1.74, or nearly one and three-quarters. By remembering these figures, and endeavoring to temper as nearly according to them as possible, the tuner will find that his temperament will come up most beautifully. This is one of the features that is over-looked or entirely unknown to many fairly good tuners; their aim being to get all fifths the same.

Finishing up the Temperament.—If your last trial, F–C, does not prove a correct fifth, you must consider how best to rectify. The following are the causes which result in improper tempera-ment:

1. Fifths too flat.
2. Fifths not flat enough.
3. Some fifths correctly tempered and others not.
4. Some fifths sharper instead of flatter than perfect; a condition that must be watched with vigi-lance.
5. Some or all of the strings tuned fall from the pitch at which they were left.

From a little reflection upon these causes, it is seen that the last trial may prove a correct fifth and yet the temperament be imperfect. If this is the case, it will be necessary to go all over the tempera-ment again. Generally, however, after you have had a little experience, you will find the trouble in one of the first two causes above, unless it be a piano wherein the strings fall as in Cause 5. This latter cause can be ascertained in cases only where you have started from a tuning pipe or fork. Sometimes you may find that the temperament may be corrected by the alteration of but two or three tones; so it is always well to stop and examine carefully before attempting the correction. A haphazard attempt might cause much extra work.

In temperament setting by our system, if the fifths are properly tempered and the octaves are left perfect, the other intervals will need no attention, and will be found beautifully correct when used in testing.

The mistuned or tempered intervals are as follows:—

INTERVALS FLATTENED.	INTERVALS SHARPENED.
The Fifth, slightly.	The Fourth, slightly.
The Minor Third, considerably.	The Major Third, greatly.
The Minor Sixth, considerably.	The Major Sixth, greatly.

Tuning the Treble. —In tuning the treble, which is always tuned by exact octaves, from their corresponding tones within the temperament, the ear will often accept an octave as true before its pitch has been sufficiently raised. Especially is

this true in the upper octaves. After tuning a
string in the treble by its octave in the temperament,
test it as a fifth. For instance, after tuning your
first string beyond the temperament, 3C♯, test it as a
fifth to 2F♯. If you are yet uncertain, try it as a
major third in·the chord of A. The beats will serve
you as a guide in testing by fifths, up to about an
octave and a half above the highest tone of the temperament; but beyond this point they become so
rapid as to be only discernible as degrees of rough-
ness. The beats will serve as a guide in tuning
octaves higher in the treble than the point at which
the beats of the *fifth* become unavailable; and in
tuning *unisons*, the beats are discernible almost to
the last tone.

The best method to follow in tuning the treble
may be summed up as follows: Tune the first
octave with the beats as guides both in the octave and
in testing it by the fifth. If yet uncertain, test by
chords. Above this octave, rely somewhat upon the
beats in the octave, still use the fifth for testing, but
listen for the pitch in the extreme upper tones and
not so much for the beats except in bringing up
unisons, in which the beats are more prominent.

In the extreme upper tones, the musical ear of the tuner is tried to the utmost. Here, his judgment of correct harmonic relation is the principal or only guide, while in the middle octaves the beats serve him so faithfully, his musical qualifications being brought into requisition only as a rough guide in determining pitch of the various intervals. To tune by the beats requires a sharp ear and mental discernment; to tune by pitch requires a fine musical ear and knowledge of the simpler laws of harmony.

As stated above, the tuner will fail in many cases to tune his high octaves sharp enough. Rarely, if ever, will a tuner with a good ear leave the upper tones too sharp. Now, there is one more fact which is of the utmost importance in tuning the treble: it is the fact that the extreme upper octave and a half must be tuned slightly sharper than perfect; if the octaves are tuned perfect, the upper tones of the instrument will sound flat when used in scale and arpeggio passages covering a large portion of the key-board. Begin to sharpen your octaves slightly from about the seventeenth key from the last; counting both black and white. In other words, begin to sharpen from the last A♭ but one, in the standard scale of seven and a third octaves of which the last key is C. Sharpen but slightly, and increase the degree of sharpening but little as you proceed.

Tuning the Bass.—In tuning the bass, listen for the beats only, in bringing up the octaves. It is sometimes well to try the string tuned, with its fifth, but the octave in the bass should suffice, as the vibrations are so much slower here that if you listen acutely the octave beats will guide you.

It is not necessary to pull the strings higher than the pitch at which they are to stand. Learn to pull them up gradually and in a way that will "render" the string over the bridges, which is an easy thing to do, the strings being so much heavier here than elsewhere. Never leave a bass string the slightest amount too sharp. As flatness is so obnoxious in the treble, just so is sharpness in the bass, so if there must be any variation in any bass tone let it be flat; but aim at perfect octaves throughout the bass.

False Waves.—We say "false waves" for want of a better name. You will find a string occasionally that will give forth waves or beats so similar to the real ones that it takes a practiced ear to distinguish the difference. Where a unison contains a string of this kind, select some other string by which to tune the interval, and leave the bad string until the last; you may then find difficulty in being able to tell when you have it in unison. The cause may be a twisted string, a fault in the string by imperfect drawing of the wire, or in the construction of the sound-board.

In the low bass tones, a kind of false waves are always present, and will annoy the tuner long after he has been in regular practice. They are, however, of a different nature from the true waves in that they are of a metallic timbre and of much greater rapidity than the latter. Close attention will generally enable the tuner to distinguish between them. They are caused by what is known as "harmonics" or "over-tones"; the string vibrating in fractional segments.

False waves will occur in an annoying degree when the tuner sets a mute on a nodal point in the string; it will cause the muted string to sound a real harmonic tone. This does not happen in the upright, as the mutes are set so near the end of the string as to preclude this possibility. In the square, how-ever, it very frequently happens, as there are so many nodes between the dampers and the bridge, where the tuner sets his mutes. If, for instance, he is tuning an octave and has his mute set precisely in the middle of the vibrating segment, in place of muting the string it sounds its own octave, which will disturb the ear in listening for the tone from the one free string. Move the mute either way until it is found to mute the string entirely.

QUESTIONS ON LESSON XIV.

1. Explain the cause of the beats.
2. How many *beats* per second in a unison of two strings, one tuned to 100, the other to 101 vibrations per second?
3. How many beats per second in an octave, the lower tone of which is tuned to 100, the upper to 201 vibrations per second?
4. How many beats per second in a fifth, the fundamental of which is tuned to 100, the fifth to 151?
5. The fifth, 2F–3C, when properly tempered, should beat 1¾ times per second. How often should a fifth, an octave higher, beat?

LESSON XV.

MISCELLANEOUS TOPICS PERTAINING TO THE PRACTICAL WORK OF TUNING, REGULATING, AND REPAIRING.

Comparison of the Different Systems.—Up to this time, we have given no account of any system of tuning except the one recommended. For the purpose of making the student more thoroughly informed we detail here several different systems which have been devised and practiced by other tuners. It is a matter of history that artisans in this profession and leaders in musical science have endeavored to devise a system of temperament having all the desirable qualifications.

The aims of many have been to invent a system which uses the fewest number of tones; working under the impression that the fewer the tones used in the temperament, the easier the tuner's work. These have reduced the compass of the temperament to the twelve semi-tones from middle C to B above; or from F below, to E above middle C.

This system requires the tuner to make use of both fourths and fifths. Not only does he have to use these two kinds of intervals in tuning, but he has to tune by fourths up and fourths down, and, likewise, by fifths up and fifths down. When tuning a fifth upward, he flattens it; and when tuning a fifth downward he sharpens the lower tone; when tuning a fourth upward, he sharpens it; when tuning a fourth downward, he flattens the lower tone.

It is readily seen that by a system of this kind the tuner's mind is constantly on a strain to know how to temper the interval he is tuning, and how much to temper it, as fourths require a different degree of tempering from the fifths; and he is constantly changing from an interval upward to one downward; so, this system must be stamped as tedious and complicated, to say the least. Yet this system is much followed in factories for rough tuning, and also by many old professional tuners.

The table on the following page gives the succession of intervals generally taken by tuners employing this system using the tones within the F octave mentioned above. Middle C is obtained in the usual way, from the tuning fork.

SYSTEM A.

By middle C tune	F	fifth below.		Temper sharp.	
By F	"	B♭(A#)	fourth above.	"	"
" C	"	G	fourth below.	"	flat
" G	"	D	fifth above.	"	"
" D	"	A	fourth below.	"	"
" A	"	E	fifth above.	"	"
" E	"	B	fourth below.	"	"
" B	"	F#	fourth below.	"	"
" F#	"	C#	fifth above.	"	"
" C#	"	G#	fourth below.	"	"
" G#	"	D#	fifth above.	"	"

Then try D# with A# previously tuned for "wolves."

We think a little study and trial of this system will produce the conviction that it is a very difficult and precarious one, and that it has every disadvantage but one, namely, that it uses the smallest possible number of tones, which is really of little value, and does not compensate for the difficulty encountered and the uncertainty of the results.

Another system which has many advantages over the above, is one which employs fifths only and covers a compass of an octave and a half. This system is similar to ours in that it employs fifths in the same succession as far as G#, the most of them, however, being an octave higher. From this G#

there is a break in the succession, and the tuner
goes back to middle C from which he started and
tunes by fifths downward until he reaches the G♯ at
which he left off.   This system employs the tones
from F below middle C to C, octave above.   Below
is the succession, starting upon 3C, whose pitch is
determined as usual.

SYSTEM B.

By 3C tune 2C   octave below.
" 2C   "   2G   fifth above.
" 2G   "   1G   octave below.
" 1G   "   2D   fifth above.
" 2D   "   2A   fifth above.
" 2A   "   1A   octave below.
" 1A   "   2E   fifth above.
" 2E   "   2B   fifth above.
" 2B   "   1B   octave below.
" 1B   "   2F♯ fifth above.
" 2F♯ "   1F♯ octave below.
" 1F♯ "   2C♯ fifth above.
" 2C♯ "   2G♯ fifth above.
" 2G♯ "   1G♯ octave below.

────────────

By 2C tune 1F   fifth below.   Temper sharp.
" 1F   "   2F   octave above.
" 2F   "   1B♭ fifth below.   Temper sharp.
" 1B♭ "   2B♭ octave above.
" 2B♭ "   2E♭ fifth below.   Temper sharp.
Now by 2E♭ try 1A♭ (G♯) fifth below for the "wolf."

Note that this last trial brings you back to the last tone
tuned before the break.

This system is used by a great number of very successful tuners, and it has but one appreciable disadvantage, which is that involved in changing from fifths upward to fifths downward. This difficulty is easily overcome, if it were all there is to encounter; but in practice, we find that after tuning the intervals in the above succession down to the last step in the first series, middle C will often have changed pitch somewhat, and the last five tones with their octaves tuned from it will not be in true harmony with the intervals tuned in the first series. For this reason it is better to go on through, as in our system, tuning by fifths upward, and if there is any change of pitch in the first tones tuned, they may be more easily corrected by going over them in the same way as at the start; also, the amount of difficulty in locating discrepancies is greatly lessened.

SYSTEM C.

The following system is one that is followed by many good tuners of the present day and has many advantages. To use this system successfully, however, one must be familiar with the number of beats necessary in each interval used.

Take 1F as a standard.

By 1F, tune 2C, fifth above.

By 1F, tune 1Bb, fourth above.

By 1F, tune 1A, major third above.

By 1F, tune 2D, sixth above.

By 1F, tune 1Ab, minor third above.

By 1F, tune 2F, octave above.

By 2C or 2D, tune 1G, fourth or fifth below.

By 1G, 1A or 2C, tune 2E, sixth, fifth or third above.

By 1G or 2E, tune 1B, third above or fourth below.

By 1A or A#, tune 2C#, major or minor third above.

By 1Ab, 1Bb or 1B, tune 2Eb, fifth, fourth or major third above.

By 1Bb, 1B, 2C# or 2Eb, tune 1F#, major third, fourth, fifth or sixth below.

As each step is taken in this system, the tone tuned is tested with any or all of the tones previously tuned.

You will notice that six tones are tuned by the first standard, F. Therefore, if any error is left in any one of the intervals it exists in this only and is not transmitted to other tones, if corrected before such other tones are used to tune by.

The numerous tests possible, early in the system, and the small compass used, one octave, may be said to be the chief advantages of the system.

The intervals used are the minor and major third, perfect fourth and fifth, and major sixth. The thirds and sixths beat from about 7 to nearly 12 per second. The exact number of beats for each step in the system may be calculated from the "Table of Vibration Numbers" in Lesson XIII. For instance, take middle C (2C) at 256, and its major third, 2E. The exact third, determined by multiplying 256 by $\frac{5}{4}$, is found to be 320. By reference to the table, we find the tempered third vibrates 322.54. The difference then is 2.54 vibrations per second, and, knowing that a difference of one vibration from the exact major third produces 4 beats, we simply multiply 2.54 by 4 and we have 10.16, the number of beats we should hear per second when this third is tempered correctly. Other intervals may be figured out in like manner by reference to the various tables given.

It is very doubtful if a beginner could succeed with this system. He should tune by an easier system until he can hear the beats very distinctly and judge quite accurately the rapidity of them. Having acquired this ability, he may try this system and follow it in preference to others.

In any system used it is well to test your work in the following manner:

Begin with your lowest major third and strike each third in succession, ascending chromatically. Of course, each third should beat slightly faster than the one below it. For instance, in our system of two octaves, take 1C–E; this third should beat about 5 per second. Next, take 1C#–F, which should beat about $5\frac{1}{2}$ per second. The beats should increase each test nearly a half beat, or the amount of 5 beats in this octave; hence, 2C–E will beat about 10 per second; or, using the exact figures, 10.16. After arriving at the last-named test, 2C–E, you may test the remainder of the two octaves by tenths, beginning with 1C–2E. The tenth is similar to the third mathematically, and its beats are even more distinct.

We may remark here that our system may be reduced to the compass of an octave and a half by simply not tuning the octaves upward which reach beyond 2F# ; and if anything were to be gained and nothing lost by shortening the compass of the temperament, we would advise using only the octave and a half. But in many years of experience in tuning all imaginable types, styles and kinds of pianos, and by all systems, we have found good reasons for adopting the two-octave temperament as laid down in Lesson VIII, for universal application. Its advantages may be summed up as follows:

Simplicity.—But two kinds of intervals are employed: the fifth and the octave. The fifth is always tuned to a fundamental below and hence always flattened, which relieves the tuner of any mental operation to determine which way he is to temper. Being a regular succession of fifths and octaves, without a break, the system is easily learned, and can be followed with little mental strain.

Uniformity.—After the tuner has become well trained in tempering his fifths, there is little danger of an uneven temperament, as the various intervals used in trials will prove a false member in some chord in time to correct it before he has gotten so far from it as to make the correction difficult. When a correction is necessary, the offending point is most easily found.

Precision.—In our experience, we have never known another system by which we could attain the absolute precision gained by this.

Stability.—Stability is the feature wherein rests the paramount reason for employing two octaves. From what has been said in previous lessons concerning the liability of some strings to flatten or sharpen by reason of altering the tension of other strings, the student will readily see that the temperament should cover a sufficient portion of the instrument, if possible, to insure that it will stand while the remaining portion is being tuned. Our two octaves cover nearly all the strings between the over-strung bass and the brace in the metal plate. This being the case, any reasonable alteration of the strings beyond, or outside, the braces from the temperament, will rarely, if ever, affect it noticeably.

Final Inspection.—Always test every key on the piano, or especially those of the middle five octaves, for bad unisons. Upon finding one, search for the string that has stood in tune, by testing each string of the unison with its octave. This being done, simply bring the other to it. Go over the whole key-board, striking octaves, and correct any that might offend. One extremely bad tone or octave may disparage your reputation, when in reality your work merits commendation.

Loose Pins.—You will occasionally find pianos in which the tuning pins have become so loose that they will not resist the pull of the strings. If many of them are in this condition it is better, before you begin to tune, to take a hammer of considerable weight and drive them a little. Commence at one end of the row of pins and aim to strike all the pins with the same force. Those which are tight enough will not yield to the blow, while those which are loose may require two or three blows to tighten them sufficiently. This defect is generally found in very old squares or cheap uprights wherein the pin-block is of poor material or defective in manufacture or in pianos which have been abused.

Split Bridges.—Even in pianos of the highest grade, we sometimes find a string sounding as if there was a pin or some metallic substance bearing against it. In such cases, find the string and examine the place where it crosses the bridge. You will often find the bridge split at that point or the bridge-pin, having yielded to the pressure of the string, vibrates against the next pin, giving rise to the singing effect. You can do little if anything toward repairing a split bridge. You may, however, stop the singing by inserting the point of your screw-driver between the close pins and pressing them apart. This will generally stop the difficulty for the time being at least.

Strings crossing the bridge near a split will not stand in tune well, and will, perhaps, have to be gone over two or three times. The same may be said of a broken metal plate. Many old squares have broken plates; generally found near the over-strung bass, or within the first octave of the treble. All the tuner can do is to apprise the owner of the defect and inform her that it will not stand well at this point, as the intense strain is thrown largely upon the wooden frame, which will have a tendency to yield gradually to it.

Stringing.—Strings break while the tuner is drawing them up, sometimes because he does not pull them gradually, gives them an abrupt turn or draws them too far above the pitch at which they are in-tended to stand. More often, however, they break from being rusty at the point where they pass over the bridge or around the tuning pin. The best in-struction concerning putting on new strings is, fol-low appearances. Make the string you put on look just like those on the instrument.   In most modern pianos the string is wound with three coils around the pin.

You will, of course, have to take out the action; not the key-board, however, unless it be one of those rare cases where the key-board and upper action are built to come out together.   In the square it is only necessary to remove the shade over the dampers, and the dampers, which are all removed easily by taking out the screw at the left.   This allows the whole set of dampers with their support to come out together.

Treble strings are nearly always passed around the hitch-pin, one wire thus forming two strings. Take out the old string, noticing how it passes over and under the felt at the dead end.   After removing the string always give the pin about three turns backward to draw it out sufficiently so that when a new string is put on, the pin will turn into the block as far as it did originally.   Run one end of the string barely through the hole in the tuning pin and turn it about twice around, taking pains that the coils lie closely; then unwind enough wire (of the same size of course) from your supply to reach down to the hitch pin and back.   Place the string on the bridge

pins properly, draw it as tight as you can by hand and
cut it off about three fingers' width beyond the pin
upon which it is to be wound. This will make about
three coils around the pin. Place the end in the hole
and turn up gradually, watching that the string is
clear down on hitch pin and properly laid on the
bridge. New strings will require drawing up two
or three times before they will stand in tune, and even

KNOT FOR SPLICING WIRE.

then they will run down in a short time. It is well
on this account to leave them slightly sharp, calling
the owner's attention to the fact.

When a bass string breaks at the point where it
starts around the tuning pin, it can nearly always be
spliced and the trouble of sending it away to have a
new one made be avoided. Take a piece of new
wire as large or larger than the old string and splice

it to the broken end by a good secure knot. A knot called the square or ruft knot is the best for this purpose. When a bass string breaks too far from the pin to permit of a splice, the only resort will be to send the broken string to some factory and have a new one made from it.

QUESTIONS ON LESSON XV.

1. Name the advantages and disadvantages of system A.
2. Name the advantages and disadvantages of system B.
3. What are the important points to be desired in any system of setting temperament?
4. State three or four items of importance in the operation of putting on a new string.
5. Why do pianos get out of tune?

LESSON XVI.

TUNING AND REPAIRING THE REED ORGAN.

An impression seems to be prevalent among some musicians of the more advanced class, that the reed organ has gone or is going out of use; in certain communities there appears to be sufficient ground for such an impression; in other communities, however, we find the number of organs largely in excess of the number of pianos. Not only is this the case, but statistics of the various organ factories throughout the United States show that the output is enormous, which is a sufficient assurance that the reed organ is not an obsolete instrument by any means. To be sure, the organ has been superseded in numerous cases by the piano, which is, in many respects, a greatly superior instrument, and, generally speaking, is more popular; yet, the reed organ has its special features of tone quality and adaptation, which render it even more desirable to many than the piano, aside from the fact of its being less expensive.

The musical effects possible on the organ and not on the piano may be few; but they are of no small value, when certain kinds of musical compositions are to be rendered.

One great point in favor of the organ is, that it is capable of continuing any tone or chord for any length of time, without diminution, while in the piano, the bass tones may be continued for considerable time, the middle tones a shorter length of time, and the extreme high tones of the treble have but the slightest duration; every tone in the piano gradually grows weaker from the instant of its sounding until it fades into silence. Another feature of the organ, not possible in the piano, is its ability of making the "crescendo" (a gradual increase of strength or volume) in single tones or chords. Still another point in favor of the organ (not in the tuner's favor, however) is that it rarely gets out of tune and does not require being gone over by the tuner at short intervals in order to keep it in fit condition to be used.

The idea with which we desire to impress the student by the foregoing remarks is, that while the piano is a superior instrument, and the art of tuning the piano is a much deeper study from the general tuner's standpoint than that of doing the various things the tuner is called to do on the organ, he should not consider the reed organ of minor importance, or slight the organ when called upon to put it in order. The fact is, persons having organs in their homes cherish them as much as others do their pianos, and there is no reason why they should not have as good service.

It will be impossible to give anything more than general instruction in organ work, as the difference in construction is so pronounced. Pianos are built practically on the same plan, and when the construction of one is learned, the tuner will find little difficulty in others of the same type; but it seems that every organ manufacturer has his own hobbies as to the best means of securing results; however, the general principles are the same, and, like many operations coming under the hand of the tuner, all that is necessary is to examine, reason, and use good mechanical judgment.

CLEANING.

Organs need cleaning about once a year, or oftener if they are kept and used in dusty places. The bellows are suction or exhaustion bellows, and they draw the air in at the top of the organ through the reeds and discharge it below. The effect of this is that if any dust is floating in the air it is drawn in about the action and reeds, where it settles and clogs the working parts, stopping the vibration of the reeds entirely.

The front board or key strip is usually held in place by a screw at each end, but sometimes by slides entering the holes in the side of the case, which may be disconnected by wooden buttons at each end, which are pulled toward the center. The back of all organs may be entered by removing the board at the back of the case, held in place by screws or buttons. Close all the stops, then take your dust blower, if you have one, or a cloth, and remove all the dirt possible in this way. Lift the muffler boards worked by the right knee-swell, take a brush and clean thoroughly next to the reeds which will be exposed when the muffler boards are raised.

If any dirt is left here it will be drawn into the reeds the instant the organ is played. In bad cases, in fact it is better in every case, to draw every reed, letting them lie in a row on the reed board and going over each one separately, brush the dust from it. This will improve the tone, or, rather, the tune of the instrument. Dirt on the tongue of a reed adds sufficient weight to alter the pitch, and if it is removed, the instrument will generally be in as good tune as when it left the factory. Simply cleaning an organ in this way is often called tuning, by inexperienced persons. If it happens that there are only a few reeds that do not speak, and the owner does not care to pay for a thorough cleaning, you will find the silent reeds by the method given under the head "Examination," and, drawing them, clean and replace.

STOPS.

Each stop on the organ (if there be no dummies) affects either the tone quality or the power of the instrument. The Vox Humana stop affects the quality of the tone by operating a fan in the rear of the instrument or a contrivance contained in a small box, which produces a tremolo effect. All other stops may be said to affect the power. Stops having such names as Diapason, Melodia, Dulcet, Celeste, Cremona, Echo, Principal, Bourdon, Sub Bass, Piccolo, Flute, Dulciana, etc., etc., open certain sets of reeds supposed to give forth a tone quality similar to the instrument whose name it bears, or the tone of the key or two must be removed to get at it. To re-move a key, take off the strip at the back of the keys, held in place by small screws, and the key may be lifted up. Now, finding the sticking pin, pull it out and sandpaper or rub it with black lead until it is found to work quite freely in the guide hole of the guide board and the hole in the reed board.

Just under the reed board is a wooden slip cov-ered with soft leather, called the valve or pallet, which covers the openings in the reed board which ad-mit air to pass down through the reeds. The tracker pin, pushed down by the key, opens the pallet which is held against the reed board by a spring and kept in place by a guide pin at each end. It sometimes happens that a pallet will be pushed down so far as to catch on the guide pins and cause the tone to sound continually. In other cases a piece of dirt will get in the way of the pallet and prevent it from closing the opening. If this be the case, draw the reeds that sound when this key is depressed and also a reed at each side of it, and pump the bellows briskly, at the same time pressing the three keys. This will generally create enough air to remove the obstacle. If the key still sounds and cannot be made to

pipes of the pipe organ bearing such names. These stops operate on the sets of reeds by raising the mutes which, when closed, stop the passage of air through the reeds.

The octave coupler stop, sometimes called Har-monique, controls an arrangement whereby, when a key is depressed, its octave is made to sound also. "Forte" stops lift the mufflers or swells, and as these are controlled by the right knee-swell, the Forte stop may be considered of little value. The left knee-swell, called the Full Organ swell, as its name im-plies, opens up the full power of all sets of reeds and throws on the couplers.

A mere peep into any organ will disclose the me-chanical working of stops, which is in such great variety that we will not attempt to detail it here.

EXAMINATION.

After a little experience you will be able to make an examination of an organ and tell just what it needs without so much as drawing a screw. The reeds are usually divided into treble sets and bass sets; two octaves of bass reeds, and three octaves of treble reeds constitute a set. The Diapason stop is nearly always present, and controls the heaviest reeds in the bass except the Bourdon or Sub Bass, if the organ should have either of these.   In examining an organ, close all stops but the Diapason, for instance, then successively press every key in the two bass octaves.

Now if, for instance, a key is found silent, that is, just an octave from the lowest tone, by counting the keys from the lowest tone, you will find the silent key is number thirteen.   Look into the organ, find the mute that is up by reason of this Diapason stop's being pulled, and count the reeds from the lowest to the thirteenth; pull the reed and you will find it obstructed or perhaps broken.   Most organs have a Dulciana stop in the treble which corresponds with the Diapason in the bass.   Test the reeds of this set just as you did those of the Diapason.   Go over each set of reeds in like manner.   Broken reeds should be sent to the factory where the organ was built.   The manufacturers will send a new one, often without cost.

Stops are sometimes found disconnected from the mutes, which deprives the player of the use of certain sets of reeds, and while it is a small matter

to connect them, it adds much to the improvemen imparted to the instrument by the tuner.   Afte: disconnecting the stops for any purpose, always be sure you connect them properly before leaving your work.

STICKING KEYS.

The key itself is subject to many of the same faults as is that of the piano.   It may bind in the guide pin or warp so as to cause it to stick, or it may stick from some substance between the keys.   Sometimes the front board is so near the front of the keys that when the latter are depressed they stick against it.   A screw is generally found in the center, the head of which comes against the front board and holds it out.   If the board is too near give the screw a turn or two back.   If there is no screw, place a piece of card against the board and the case at the ends. The end keys sometimes stick against the blocks at the ends of the key-board.   Scrape the block or key where it sticks.   A key may stay down because of the cedar pin, sometimes called the tracker pin or pitman, sticking in the hole.   Take out the key-board which is held by a screw at each end, sometimes by another in the middle; in which case a

"hush up" in this way, you may be compelled to take out the entire action so that you can get to the pallets, which can be done by removing all the screws that hold the reed board in place. At the back, these screws are on top of the board and sometimes they are on top in front; but often they are under the air chamber in front. Be sure the screws are all out before trying to pull the board loose, as you might crack the board and thereby cause a leak. A moment's notice will reveal the cause of the trouble in the pallet.

New pallet springs may be made of piano wire, using old springs for a pattern.

Leaks.

If a leak is found in the air boards, such as a crack or split, it can be stopped permanently by gluing a piece of bellows cloth or any good rubber cloth over the split. A leak in the bellows can be repaired in the same way, but if it happens to be a hole at or near a part of the cloth which is compelled to bend in the working of the bellows, you will have to use some kind of rubber or leather cement, preferably the latter. This can be made by dissolving gutta-percha in bisulphide of carbon, but a good leather cement may be had at almost any shoe store. If the bellows are porous, it may be well to give them a coat of cement, but never paint them; the paint cracks and the leaks are made worse.

PEDAL DEFECTS.

Broken pedal straps are the most frequent annoyance. In all modern organs there is a panel above the pedals which will come out and admit the mechanic to the bellows, straps, springs, etc.; but in some old instruments the case is made solid, in which case the workman must do his work from the bottom, turning the organ down so as to get at it. Pedal straps are easily put on; generally with screws at either end. If the pedal squeaks examine the springs or oil and change their position slightly. Examine the pulleys over which the straps work and oil or rub them on the outside with soap. Broken pedal hinges may be duplicated by any blacksmith; the ordinary hinges, such as can be bought at hardware stores, are sometimes substituted, but they rarely answer the purpose as well as the regular pedal hinge. The leather flaps over the holes in the exhausters sometimes get too tight by shrinkage so that they will not let the air escape readily, and consequently the pedals come up slowly, often making it difficult to keep the instrument sufficiently supplied with power. Simply stretch the leather flaps, being careful not to pull the tacks loose or tear the leather.

SYMPATHETIC VIBRATIONS.

Organs, like pianos, are subject to sympathetic vibrations. A reed fitting loosely in the reed chamber will sometimes buzz when sounded. A bit of paper under the back end of the reed will stop it. Any loose material about the instrument may cause trouble of this kind. Trace up the cause and the remedy will suggest itself.

A buzzing sound may be caused by a reed's being too tight in the reed chamber, causing the tongue to vibrate against the sides of the brass body. In some rare cases, not being firmly riveted, the tongue will move to one side, causing the same trouble. Care and pains must be taken in working with reeds, but when in this condition they must be repaired. Tap the rivet lightly with a hammer and try it; if it still does not sound clear, catch the butt of the reed (riveted end) with a pair of parallel pliers, and turn it toward the center until, when vibrating, it clears the jaws.

TUNING.

The method of tuning the organ is very simple. To flatten the tone of a reed, scrape the tongue near the butt or rivet, making it thinner at that point, which will cause it to vibrate at a slower rate. To sharpen the tone, scrape it at the point, thereby lightening the vibrating end, which will cause a more rapid rate of vibration. When a reed has been scraped or filed so thin at the point that it will bear no more scraping, it can sometimes be sharpened by bending it up and down a few times, which has a tendency to put temper in the metal. Some reeds are curved at the point purposely to secure a certain voice. Do not interfere with the proper curvature when tuning. In tuning organs, the same system and general instruction given for piano tuning will apply; however, it is rarely, if ever, necessary to give an organ as thorough tuning as you would a piano. It is a very tedious job where you have to draw each reed, apply the proper method, insert it and try the result, thus cutting and trying each one perhaps several times before getting the desired result. In factories devices are used which render the operation very much easier.

One thing you should know is, that organs are not tempered as finely as pianos, nor is there the pains taken to secure perfect unisons. In fact, you can hardly find a perfect unison in an organ of modern make, much less, a correct temperament. Finding a tone that is so far out as to be very disagreeable, adjust it between the octave below and the octave above, try it in the proper chords and equalize it in the best possible way; but it is not often you will be able to tune it to absolute precision with its octaves. It is thought by many that a slight deviation from correct unisons, sufficient to give a series of waves, gives the organ a more mellow voice and consequently a more musical (?) tone; and while we do not agree with any such proposition, it makes the tuner's work less exacting.

We feel that an apology is in order for not giving illustrations of the action of the organ, but if the student will study this lesson in connection with the instrument itself, we believe he will have no trouble in learning all about its mechanical action and its demands upon the tuner.

QUESTIONS ON LESSON XVI.

1. Name the musical advantages possessed by the organ which are absent in the piano.

2. Name the musical advantages possessed by the piano which are absent in the organ.

3. Describe the mechanical operations taking place in the organ when a key is being sounded.

4. State what you would do to flatten the tone of a reed and give reasons.

5. State what you would do to sharpen the tone of a reed and give reasons.

LESSON XVII.

CONCLUDING PROFESSIONAL HINTS.

Peculiar incidents occur in the experience of the piano tuner, some of which have come under the observation of the author so frequently that he deems it advisable to mention them here; there are incidents also that happen once in a life-time which must be treated in their time with tact and good judgment, and which it is impossible to describe here, as each tuner, in his special field, will elicit new developments. Occasion often requires the tuner to summon all his wits and tact in order to dispose of questions put to him, both by pianos and owners.

Among the perplexing things that come to the tuner are the terms used by musicians and piano owners to express certain qualities of tone and certain discrepancies of the instrument. We will define a number of these.

Brilliant.—The sense in which this term is used is astonishing to one who is accustomed to using words according to their dictionary meanings. We have heard persons say their piano was too *brilliant;* or, that it was not *brilliant* enough. They mean this term to apply to what we are pleased to call the voice of the instrument. When the hammers are hard, producing a sharp, penetrating tone, they call it *brilliant;* when the hammers are soft and produce what a trained ear would accept as a soft, sweet, musical tone, some persons will say that the instrument lacks brilliancy. Persons of a different taste, and, we would say, a more cultured ear, call the tone *harsh* when the hammers are hard, and they usually desire the tuner to *soften* the tone, which he does by softening the hammer ends as has been described in Lesson VII. This operation, which we call voicing, is a very delicate piece of work, and the tuner should exercise care and pains in doing it; so we will deviate from the trend of the discourse and offer a few directions here, as the previous instructions are hardly complete.

Insert the felt pick (which should contain only one point, and not three or four, as they usually do) in the point of the hammer and give it a rotary motion, so to speak, loosening up the felt and giving it its original elasticity. Do not pick up the felt at the point. This method, which is resorted to by many tuners, is injurious to the hammers and really does no permanent good. Another method which is very good, and a very easy one, is to take your parallel pliers and squeeze the felt slightly at the point. Apply the pliers at right angles with the hammer (if the action of the upright, your pliers will be in an upright position) and catch the hammer at a depth of about three-quarters of the thickness of the felt. If the hammers are very hard it may be well to use both the pliers and the pick; but care must always be taken not to get the hammers too soft, and extreme care must be taken not to get some softer than others. Some hammers are always used more than others and, of course, these will need more softening. Usually those at the extreme ends of the instrument will need no softening at all, but sometimes the bass will bear considerable softening. After going over them in the above way, try them by playing the chromatic scale and you will invariably find some that need additional attention. Be sure that no hard tone is left, as such a condition is a great annoyance to a delicate ear.

Singing.—When a damper is out of order and does not do its work properly, they often say the tone *sings*. They say the same thing about the reed organ when a pallet sticks or a key stays down. Sometimes this term is used to express the grating vibration which has been treated under the head of *sympathetic rattle*.

Tin-panny.—This term is often used and generally means that the instrument is out of tune, and especially that the unisons are out. Sometimes it is used to express a *hollow* quality of tone; but you will rarely, if ever, hear a piano spoken of in this way if it is in correct tune. Any piano out of tune badly may be said to sound tin-panny.

Bass-ey.—This term expresses a very harsh bass. Imperfect octaves or unisons in the bass of a piano give rise to the use of this term. If the bass of the instrument is decidedly flat, the same term is sometimes used to express the condition.

Harsh.—This term, when it does not apply to the voice of the piano, generally reflects upon the work of the tuner (?). Chords are *harsh* when they contain over-sharp thirds, bad fifths, octaves, etc. Take care that your temperament contains no bad chords, and after you are all through, see that all tones have stood, and that you have left no bad unisons or octaves.   One or two carelessly tuned tonse may disparage your otherwise creditable work.

Questions.—Questions are often asked the tuner concerning the care of the piano.   Be prepared to answer any reasonable question that may come up, which your knowledge of the instrument should enable you to do.   In regard to temperature, moisture, etc., an extreme either way is the thing to avoid.   A very dry or hot atmosphere will crack the varnish, warp the wooden parts, crack the sound-board, cause parts to come unglued, etc.   On the other hand, too much moisture will rust the steel parts, strings, etc.; so the "happy medium" is the condition to be desired.   As to keeping pianos closed, a question you will often be asked, we think it is better to keep them open at all times than to keep them closed at all times; because, if they are kept open they are subjected to the changes of the atmosphere, which will rarely permit the piano to become either very damp or too dry.   In a word, a room that is healthy for human beings is all right for the piano.

Seasons for Tuning.—The prevalent idea in regard to this matter is that pianos should be tuned either at the beginning of cold or of warm weather. In our experience, we have found that it makes no difference when the piano is tuned if it is kept in the living room. If, however, a piano were tuned upon a warm day in the fall and then allowed to remain in a room in which the temperature suddenly fell to zero, we could not expect it to stand in tune; and much less, if the room is heated up occasionally and then left for an interval at the mercy of the weather. Persons who treat their pianos in this way should have them tuned about four times a year.

INDEX.

A CATALOGUE OF SELECTED DOVER BOOKS
IN ALL FIELDS OF INTEREST

A CATALOGUE OF SELECTED DOVER BOOKS
IN ALL FIELDS OF INTEREST

AMERICA'S OLD MASTERS, James T. Flexner. Four men emerged unexpectedly from provincial 18th century America to leadership in European art: Benjamin West, J. S. Copley, C. R. Peale, Gilbert Stuart. Brilliant coverage of lives and contributions. Revised, 1967 edition. 69 plates. 365pp. of text.

21806-6 Paperbound $3.00

FIRST FLOWERS OF OUR WILDERNESS: AMERICAN PAINTING, THE COLONIAL PERIOD, James T. Flexner. Painters, and regional painting traditions from earliest Colonial times up to the emergence of Copley, West and Peale Sr., Foster, Gustavus Hesselius, Feke, John Smibert and many anonymous painters in the primitive manner. Engaging presentation, with 162 illustrations. xxii + 368pp.

22180-6 Paperbound $3.50

THE LIGHT OF DISTANT SKIES: AMERICAN PAINTING, 1760-1835, James T. Flexner. The great generation of early American painters goes to Europe to learn and to teach: West, Copley, Gilbert Stuart and others. Allston, Trumbull, Morse; also contemporary American painters—primitives, derivatives, academics—who remained in America. 102 illustrations. xiii + 306pp. 22179-2 Paperbound $3.50

A HISTORY OF THE RISE AND PROGRESS OF THE ARTS OF DESIGN IN THE UNITED STATES, William Dunlap. Much the richest mine of information on early American painters, sculptors, architects, engravers, miniaturists, etc. The only source of information for scores of artists, the major primary source for many others. Unabridged reprint of rare original 1834 edition, with new introduction by James T. Flexner, and 394 new illustrations. Edited by Rita Weiss. 6⅝ x 9⅝.

21695-0, 21696-9, 21697-7 Three volumes, Paperbound $15.00

EPOCHS OF CHINESE AND JAPANESE ART, Ernest F. Fenollosa. From primitive Chinese art to the 20th century, thorough history, explanation of every important art period and form, including Japanese woodcuts; main stress on China and Japan, but Tibet, Korea also included. Still unexcelled for its detailed, rich coverage of cultural background, aesthetic elements, diffusion studies, particularly of the historical period. 2nd, 1913 edition. 242 illustrations. lii + 439pp. of text.

20364-6, 20365-4 Two volumes, Paperbound $6.00

THE GENTLE ART OF MAKING ENEMIES, James A. M. Whistler. Greatest wit of his day deflates Oscar Wilde, Ruskin, Swinburne; strikes back at inane critics, exhibitions, art journalism; aesthetics of impressionist revolution in most striking form. Highly readable classic by great painter. Reproduction of edition designed by Whistler. Introduction by Alfred Werner. xxxvi + 334pp.

21875-9 Paperbound $3.00

VISUAL ILLUSIONS: THEIR CAUSES, CHARACTERISTICS, AND APPLICATIONS, Matthew Luckiesh. Thorough description and discussion of optical illusion, geometric and perspective, particularly; size and shape distortions, illusions of color, of motion; natural illusions; use of illusion in art and magic, industry, etc. Most useful today with op art, also for classical art. Scores of effects illustrated. Introduction by William H. Ittleson. 100 illustrations. xxi + 252pp.
21530-X Paperbound $2.00

A HANDBOOK OF ANATOMY FOR ART STUDENTS, Arthur Thomson. Thorough, virtually exhaustive coverage of skeletal structure, musculature, etc. Full text, supplemented by anatomical diagrams and drawings and by photographs of undraped figures. Unique in its comparison of male and female forms, pointing out differences of contour, texture, form. 211 figures, 40 drawings, 86 photographs. xx + 459pp. 5⅜ x 8⅜.
21163-0 Paperbound $3.50

150 MASTERPIECES OF DRAWING, Selected by Anthony Toney. Full page reproductions of drawings from the early 16th to the end of the 18th century, all beautifully reproduced: Rembrandt, Michelangelo, Dürer, Fragonard, Urs, Graf, Wouwerman, many others. First-rate browsing book, model book for artists. xviii + 150pp. 8⅜ x 11¼.
21032-4 Paperbound $2.50

THE LATER WORK OF AUBREY BEARDSLEY, Aubrey Beardsley. Exotic, erotic, ironic masterpieces in full maturity: Comedy Ballet, Venus and Tannhauser, Pierrot, Lysistrata, Rape of the Lock, Savoy material, Ali Baba, Volpone, etc. This material revolutionized the art world, and is still powerful, fresh, brilliant. With The Early Work, all Beardsley's finest work. 174 plates, 2 in color. xiv + 176pp. 8⅛ x 11.
21817-1 Paperbound $3.75

DRAWINGS OF REMBRANDT, Rembrandt van Rijn. Complete reproduction of fabulously rare edition by Lippmann and Hofstede de Groot, completely reedited, updated, improved by Prof. Seymour Slive, Fogg Museum. Portraits, Biblical sketches, landscapes, Oriental types, nudes, episodes from classical mythology—All Rembrandt's fertile genius. Also selection of drawings by his pupils and followers. "Stunning volumes," Saturday Review. 550 illustrations. lxxviii + 552pp. 9⅛ x 12¼.
21485-0, 21486-9 Two volumes, Paperbound $10.00

THE DISASTERS OF WAR, Francisco Goya. One of the masterpieces of Western civilization—83 etchings that record Goya's shattering, bitter reaction to the Napoleonic war that swept through Spain after the insurrection of 1808 and to war in general. Reprint of the first edition, with three additional plates from Boston's Museum of Fine Arts. All plates facsimile size. Introduction by Philip Hofer, Fogg Museum. v + 97pp. 9⅜ x 8¼.
21872-4 Paperbound $2.50

GRAPHIC WORKS OF ODILON REDON. Largest collection of Redon's graphic works ever assembled: 172 lithographs, 28 etchings and engravings, 9 drawings. These include some of his most famous works. All the plates from Odilon Redon: oeuvre graphique complet, plus additional plates. New introduction and caption translations by Alfred Werner. 209 illustrations. xxvii + 209pp. 9⅛ x 12¼.
21966-8 Paperbound $4.50

A HISTORY OF COSTUME, Carl Köhler. Definitive history, based on surviving pieces of clothing primarily, and paintings, statues, etc. secondarily. Highly readable text, supplemented by 594 illustrations of costumes of the ancient Mediterranean peoples, Greece and Rome, the Teutonic prehistoric period; costumes of the Middle Ages, Renaissance, Baroque, 18th and 19th centuries. Clear, measured patterns are provided for many clothing articles. Approach is practical throughout. Enlarged by Emma von Sichart. 464pp. 21030-8 Paperbound $3.50

ORIENTAL RUGS, ANTIQUE AND MODERN, Walter A. Hawley. A complete and authoritative treatise on the Oriental rug—where they are made, by whom and how, designs and symbols, characteristics in detail of the six major groups, how to distinguish them and how to buy them. Detailed technical data is provided on periods, weaves, warps, wefts, textures, sides, ends and knots, although no technical background is required for an understanding. 11 color plates, 80 halftones, 4 maps. vi + 320pp. $6\frac{1}{8}$ x $9\frac{1}{8}$. 22366-3 Paperbound $5.00

TEN BOOKS ON ARCHITECTURE, Vitruvius. By any standards the most important book on architecture ever written. Early Roman discussion of aesthetics of building, construction methods, orders, sites, and every other aspect of architecture has inspired, instructed architecture for about 2,000 years. Stands behind Palladio, Michelangelo, Bramante, Wren, countless others. Definitive Morris H. Morgan translation. 68 illustrations. xii + 331pp. 20645-9 Paperbound.$3.00

THE FOUR BOOKS OF ARCHITECTURE, Andrea Palladio. Translated into every major Western European language in the two centuries following its publication in 1570, this has been one of the most influential books in the history of architecture. Complete reprint of the 1738 Isaac Ware edition. New introduction by Adolf Placzek, Columbia Univ. 216 plates. xxii + 110pp. of text. $9\frac{1}{2}$ x $12\frac{3}{4}$. 21308-0 Clothbound $12.50

STICKS AND STONES: A STUDY OF AMERICAN ARCHITECTURE AND CIVILIZATION, Lewis Mumford.One of the great classics of American cultural history. American architecture from the medieval-inspired earliest forms to the early 20th century; evolution of structure and style, and reciprocal influences on environment. 21 photographic illustrations. 238pp. 20202-X Paperbound $2.00

THE AMERICAN BUILDER'S COMPANION, Asher Benjamin. The most widely used early 19th century architectural style and source book, for colonial up into Greek Revival periods. Extensive development of geometry of carpentering, construction of sashes, frames, doors, stairs; plans and elevations of domestic and other buildings. Hundreds of thousands of houses were built according to this book, now invaluable to historians, architects, restorers, etc. 1827 edition. 59 plates. 114pp. $7\frac{7}{8}$ x $10\frac{3}{4}$. 22236-5 Paperbound $4.00

DUTCH HOUSES IN THE HUDSON VALLEY BEFORE 1776, Helen Wilkinson Reynolds. The standard survey of the Dutch colonial house and outbuildings, with constructional features, decoration, and local history associated with individual homesteads. Introduction by Franklin D. Roosevelt. Map. 150 illustrations. 469pp. $6\frac{5}{8}$ x $9\frac{1}{4}$. 21469-9 Paperbound $5.00

THE ARCHITECTURE OF COUNTRY HOUSES, Andrew J. Downing. Together with Vaux's *Villas and Cottages* this is the basic book for Hudson River Gothic architecture of the middle Victorian period. Full, sound discussions of general aspects of housing, architecture, style, decoration, furnishing, together with scores of detailed house plans, illustrations of specific buildings, accompanied by full text. Perhaps the most influential single American architectural book. 1850 edition. Introduction by J. Stewart Johnson. 321 figures, 34 architectural designs. xvi + 560pp.
22003-6 Paperbound $5.00

LOST EXAMPLES OF COLONIAL ARCHITECTURE, John Mead Howells. Full-page photographs of buildings that have disappeared or been so altered as to be denatured, including many designed by major early American architects. 245 plates. xvii + 248pp. 7⅞ x 10¾. 21143-6 Paperbound $3.50

DOMESTIC ARCHITECTURE OF THE AMERICAN COLONIES AND OF THE EARLY REPUBLIC, Fiske Kimball. Foremost architect and restorer of Williamsburg and Monticello covers nearly 200 homes between 1620-1825. Architectural details, construction, style features, special fixtures, floor plans, etc. Generally considered finest work in its area. 219 illustrations of houses, doorways, windows, capital mantels. xx + 314pp. 7⅞ x 10¾. 21743-4 Paperbound $4.00

EARLY AMERICAN ROOMS: 1650-1858, edited by Russell Hawes Kettell. Tour of 12 rooms, each representative of a different era in American history and each furnished, decorated, designed and occupied in the style of the era. 72 plans and elevations, 8-page color section, etc., show fabrics, wall papers, arrangements, etc. Full descriptive text. xvii + 200pp. of text. 8⅜ x 11¼.
21633-0 Paperbound $5.00

THE FITZWILLIAM VIRGINAL BOOK, edited by J. Fuller Maitland and W. B. Squire. Full modern printing of famous early 17th-century ms. volume of 300 works by Morley, Byrd, Bull, Gibbons, etc. For piano or other modern keyboard instrument; easy to read format. xxxvi + 938pp. 8⅜ x 11.
21068-5, 21069-3 Two volumes, Paperbound $12.00

KEYBOARD MUSIC, Johann Sebastian Bach. Bach Gesellschaft edition. A rich selection of Bach's masterpieces for the harpsichord: the six English Suites, six French Suites, the six Partitas (Clavierübung part I), the Goldberg Variations (Clavierübung part IV), the fifteen Two-Part Inventions and the fifteen Three-Part Sinfonias. Clearly reproduced on large sheets with ample margins; eminently playable. vi + 312pp. 8⅛ x 11. 22360-4 Paperbound $5.00

THE MUSIC OF BACH: AN INTRODUCTION, Charles Sanford Terry. A fine, nontechnical introduction to Bach's music, both instrumental and vocal. Covers organ music, chamber music, passion music, other types. Analyzes themes, developments, innovations. x + 114pp. 21075-8 Paperbound $1.95

BEETHOVEN AND HIS NINE SYMPHONIES, Sir George Grove. Noted British musicologist provides best history, analysis, commentary on symphonies. Very thorough, rigorously accurate; necessary to both advanced student and amateur music lover. 436 musical passages. vii + 407 pp. 20334-4 Paperbound $4.00

JOHANN SEBASTIAN BACH, Philipp Spitta. One of the great classics of musicology, this definitive analysis of Bach's music (and life) has never been surpassed. Lucid, nontechnical analyses of hundreds of pieces (30 pages devoted to St. Matthew Passion, 26 to B Minor Mass). Also includes major analysis of 18th-century music. 450 musical examples. 40-page musical supplement. Total of xx + 1799pp.

(EUK) 22278-0, 22279-9 Two volumes, Clothbound $25.00

MOZART AND HIS PIANO CONCERTOS, Cuthbert Girdlestone. The only full-length study of an important area of Mozart's creativity. Provides detailed analyses of all 23 concertos, traces inspirational sources. 417 musical examples. Second edition. 509pp.

21271-8 Paperbound $4.50

THE PERFECT WAGNERITE: A COMMENTARY ON THE NIBLUNG'S RING, George Bernard Shaw. Brilliant and still relevant criticism in remarkable essays on Wagner's Ring cycle, Shaw's ideas on political and social ideology behind the plots, role of Leitmotifs, vocal requisites, etc. Prefaces. xxi + 136pp.

(USO) 21707-8 Paperbound $1.75

DON GIOVANNI, W. A. Mozart. Complete libretto, modern English translation; biographies of composer and librettist; accounts of early performances and critical reaction. Lavishly illustrated. All the material you need to understand and appreciate this great work. Dover Opera Guide and Libretto Series; translated and introduced by Ellen Bleiler. 92 illustrations. 209pp.

21134-7 Paperbound $2.00

BASIC ELECTRICITY, U. S. Bureau of Naval Personel. Originally a training course, best non-technical coverage of basic theory of electricity and its applications. Fundamental concepts, batteries, circuits, conductors and wiring techniques, AC and DC, inductance and capacitance, generators, motors, transformers, magnetic amplifiers, synchros, servomechanisms, etc. Also covers blue-prints, electrical diagrams, etc. Many questions, with answers. 349 illustrations. x + 448pp. 6½ x 9¼.

20973-3 Paperbound $3.50

REPRODUCTION OF SOUND, Edgar Villchur. Thorough coverage for laymen of high fidelity systems, reproducing systems in general, needles, amplifiers, preamps, loudspeakers, feedback, explaining physical background. "A rare talent for making technicalities vividly comprehensible," R. Darrell, *High Fidelity*. 69 figures. iv + 92pp.

21515-6 Paperbound $1.35

HEAR ME TALKIN' TO YA: THE STORY OF JAZZ AS TOLD BY THE MEN WHO MADE IT, Nat Shapiro and Nat Hentoff. Louis Armstrong, Fats Waller, Jo Jones, Clarence Williams, Billy Holiday, Duke Ellington, Jelly Roll Morton and dozens of other jazz greats tell how it was in Chicago's South Side, New Orleans, depression Harlem and the modern West Coast as jazz was born and grew. xvi + 429pp.

21726-4 Paperbound $3.95

FABLES OF AESOP, translated by Sir Roger L'Estrange. A reproduction of the very rare 1931 Paris edition; a selection of the most interesting fables, together with 50 imaginative drawings by Alexander Calder. v + 128pp. 6½x9¼.

21780-9 Paperbound $1.50

AGAINST THE GRAIN (A REBOURS), Joris K. Huysmans. Filled with weird images, evidences of a bizarre imagination, exotic experiments with hallucinatory drugs, rich tastes and smells and the diversions of its sybarite hero Duc Jean des Esseintes, this classic novel pushed 19th-century literary decadence to its limits. Full unabridged edition. Do not confuse this with abridged editions generally sold. Introduction by Havelock Ellis. xlix + 206pp. 22190-3 Paperbound $2.50

VARIORUM SHAKESPEARE: HAMLET. Edited by Horace H. Furness; a landmark of American scholarship. Exhaustive footnotes and appendices treat all doubtful words and phrases, as well as suggested critical emendations throughout the play's history. First volume contains editor's own text, collated with all Quartos and Folios. Second volume contains full first Quarto, translations of Shakespeare's sources (Belleforest, and Saxo Grammaticus), Der Bestrafte Brudermord, and many essays on critical and historical points of interest by major authorities of past and present. Includes details of staging and costuming over the years. By far the best edition available for serious students of Shakespeare. Total of xx + 905pp.
21004-9, 21005-7, 2 volumes, Paperbound $7.00

A LIFE OF WILLIAM SHAKESPEARE, Sir Sidney Lee. This is the standard life of Shakespeare, summarizing everything known about Shakespeare and his plays. Incredibly rich in material, broad in coverage, clear and judicious, it has served thousands as the best introduction to Shakespeare. 1931 edition. 9 plates. xxix + 792pp. 21967-4 Paperbound $4.50

MASTERS OF THE DRAMA, John Gassner. Most comprehensive history of the drama in print, covering every tradition from Greeks to modern Europe and America, including India, Far East, etc. Covers more than 800 dramatists, 2000 plays, with biographical material, plot summaries, theatre history, criticism, etc. "Best of its kind in English," *New Republic*. 77 illustrations. xxii + 890pp.
20100-7 Clothbound $10.00

THE EVOLUTION OF THE ENGLISH LANGUAGE, George McKnight. The growth of English, from the 14th century to the present. Unusual, non-technical account presents basic information in very interesting form: sound shifts, change in grammar and syntax, vocabulary growth, similar topics. Abundantly illustrated with quotations. Formerly *Modern English in the Making*. xii + 590pp.
21932-1 Paperbound $3.50

AN ETYMOLOGICAL DICTIONARY OF MODERN ENGLISH, Ernest Weekley. Fullest, richest work of its sort, by foremost British lexicographer. Detailed word histories, including many colloquial and archaic words; extensive quotations. Do not confuse this with the Concise Etymological Dictionary, which is much abridged. Total of xxvii + 830pp. 6½ x 9¼.
21873-2, 21874-0 Two volumes, Paperbound $7.90

FLATLAND: A ROMANCE OF MANY DIMENSIONS, E. A. Abbott. Classic of science-fiction explores ramifications of life in a two-dimensional world, and what happens when a three-dimensional being intrudes. Amusing reading, but also useful as introduction to thought about hyperspace. Introduction by Banesh Hoffmann. 16 illustrations. xx + 103pp. 20001-9 Paperbound $1.00

POEMS OF ANNE BRADSTREET, edited with an introduction by Robert Hutchinson. A new selection of poems by America's first poet and perhaps the first significant woman poet in the English language. 48 poems display her development in works of considerable variety—love poems, domestic poems, religious meditations, formal elegies, "quaternions," etc. Notes, bibliography. viii + 222pp.

22160-1 Paperbound $2.50

THREE GOTHIC NOVELS: THE CASTLE OF OTRANTO BY HORACE WALPOLE; VATHEK BY WILLIAM BECKFORD; THE VAMPYRE BY JOHN POLIDORI, WITH FRAGMENT OF A NOVEL BY LORD BYRON, edited by E. F. Bleiler. The first Gothic novel, by Walpole; the finest Oriental tale in English, by Beckford; powerful Romantic supernatural story in versions by Polidori and Byron. All extremely important in history of literature; all still exciting, packed with supernatural thrills, ghosts, haunted castles, magic, etc. xl + 291pp.

21232-7 Paperbound $3.00

THE BEST TALES OF HOFFMANN, E. T. A. Hoffmann. 10 of Hoffmann's most important stories, in modern re-editings of standard translations: Nutcracker and the King of Mice, Signor Formica, Automata, The Sandman, Rath Krespel, The Golden Flowerpot, Master Martin the Cooper, The Mines of Falun, The King's Betrothed, A New Year's Eve Adventure. 7 illustrations by Hoffmann. Edited by E. F. Bleiler. xxxix + 419pp. 21793-0 Paperbound $3.00

GHOST AND HORROR STORIES OF AMBROSE BIERCE, Ambrose Bierce. 23 strikingly modern stories of the horrors latent in the human mind: The Eyes of the Panther, The Damned Thing, An Occurrence at Owl Creek Bridge, An Inhabitant of Carcosa, etc., plus the dream-essay, Visions of the Night. Edited by E. F. Bleiler. xxii + 199pp. 20767-6 Paperbound $2.00

BEST GHOST STORIES OF J. S. LEFANU, J. Sheridan LeFanu. Finest stories by Victorian master often considered greatest supernatural writer of all. Carmilla, Green Tea, The Haunted Baronet, The Familiar, and 12 others. Most never before available in the U. S. A. Edited by E. F. Bleiler. 8 illustrations from Victorian publications. xvii + 467pp. 20415-4 Paperbound $3.00

MATHEMATICAL FOUNDATIONS OF INFORMATION THEORY, A. I. Khinchin. Comprehensive introduction to work of Shannon, McMillan, Feinstein and Khinchin, placing these investigations on a rigorous mathematical basis. Covers entropy concept in probability theory, uniqueness theorem, Shannon's inequality, ergodic sources, the E property, martingale concept, noise, Feinstein's fundamental lemma, Shanon's first and second theorems. Translated by R. A. Silverman and M. D. Friedman. iii + 120pp. 60434-9 Paperbound $2.00

SEVEN SCIENCE FICTION NOVELS, H. G. Wells. The standard collection of the great novels. Complete, unabridged. *First Men in the Moon, Island of Dr. Moreau, War of the Worlds, Food of the Gods, Invisible Man, Time Machine, In the Days of the Comet.* Not only science fiction fans, but every educated person owes it to himself to read these novels. 1015pp. (USO) 20264-X Clothbound $6.00

"ESSENTIAL GRAMMAR" SERIES

All you really need to know about modern, colloquial grammar. Many educational shortcuts help you learn faster, understand better. Detailed cognate lists teach you to recognize similarities between English and foreign words and roots—make learning vocabulary easy and interesting. Excellent for independent study or as a supplement to record courses.

ESSENTIAL FRENCH GRAMMAR, Seymour Resnick. 2500-item cognate list. 159pp.
(EBE) 20419-7 Paperbound $1.50

ESSENTIAL GERMAN GRAMMAR, Guy Stern and Everett F. Bleiler. Unusual shortcuts on noun declension, word order, compound verbs. 124pp.
(EBE) 20422-7 Paperbound $1.25

ESSENTIAL ITALIAN GRAMMAR, Olga Ragusa. 111pp.
(EBE) 20779-X Paperbound $1.25

ESSENTIAL JAPANESE GRAMMAR, Everett F. Bleiler. In Romaji transcription; no characters needed. Japanese grammar is regular and simple. 156pp.
21027-8 Paperbound $1.50

ESSENTIAL PORTUGUESE GRAMMAR, Alexander da R. Prista. vi + 114pp.
21650-0 Paperbound $1.35

ESSENTIAL SPANISH GRAMMAR, Seymour Resnick. 2500 word cognate list. 115pp.
(EBE) 20780-3 Paperbound $1.25

ESSENTIAL ENGLISH GRAMMAR, Philip Gucker. Combines best features of modern, functional and traditional approaches. For refresher, class use, home study. x + 177pp.
21649-7 Paperbound $1.75

A PHRASE AND SENTENCE DICTIONARY OF SPOKEN SPANISH. Prepared for U. S. War Department by U. S. linguists. As above, unit is idiom, phrase or sentence rather than word. English-Spanish and Spanish-English sections contain modern equivalents of over 18,000 sentences. Introduction and appendix as above. iv + 513pp.
20495-2 Paperbound $3.50

A PHRASE AND SENTENCE DICTIONARY OF SPOKEN RUSSIAN. Dictionary prepared for U. S. War Department by U. S. linguists. Basic unit is not the word, but the idiom, phrase or sentence. English-Russian and Russian-English sections contain modern equivalents for over 30,000 phrases. Grammatical introduction covers phonetics, writing, syntax. Appendix of word lists for food, numbers, geographical names, etc. vi + 573 pp. 6⅛ x 9¼.
20496-0 Paperbound $5.50

CONVERSATIONAL CHINESE FOR BEGINNERS, Morris Swadesh. Phonetic system, beginner's course in Pai Hua Mandarin Chinese covering most important, most useful speech patterns. Emphasis on modern colloquial usage. Formerly *Chinese in Your Pocket*. xvi + 158pp.
21123-1 Paperbound $1.75

HOW TO KNOW THE WILD FLOWERS, Mrs. William Starr Dana. This is the classical book of American wildflowers (of the Eastern and Central United States), used by hundreds of thousands. Covers over 500 species, arranged in extremely easy to use color and season groups. Full descriptions, much plant lore. This Dover edition is the fullest ever compiled, with tables of nomenclature changes. 174 full-page plates by M. Satterlee. xii + 418pp. 20332-8 Paperbound $3.00

OUR PLANT FRIENDS AND FOES, William Atherton DuPuy. History, economic importance, essential botanical information and peculiarities of 25 common forms of plant life are provided in this book in an entertaining and charming style. Covers food plants (potatoes, apples, beans, wheat, almonds, bananas, etc.), flowers (lily, tulip, etc.), trees (pine, oak, elm, etc.), weeds, poisonous mushrooms and vines, gourds, citrus fruits, cotton, the cactus family, and much more. 108 illustrations. xiv + 290pp. 22272-1 Paperbound $2.50

HOW TO KNOW THE FERNS, Frances T. Parsons. Classic survey of Eastern and Central ferns, arranged according to clear, simple identification key. Excellent introduction to greatly neglected nature area. 57 illustrations and 42 plates. xvi + 215pp. 20740-4 Paperbound $2.00

MANUAL OF THE TREES OF NORTH AMERICA, Charles S. Sargent. America's foremost dendrologist provides the definitive coverage of North American trees and tree-like shrubs. 717 species fully described and illustrated: exact distribution, down to township; full botanical description; economic importance; description of subspecies and races; habitat, growth data; similar material. Necessary to every serious student of tree-life. Nomenclature revised to present. Over 100 locating keys. 783 illustrations. lii + 934pp. 20277-1, 20278-X Two volumes, Paperbound $7.00

OUR NORTHERN SHRUBS, Harriet L. Keeler. Fine non-technical reference work identifying more than 225 important shrubs of Eastern and Central United States and Canada. Full text covering botanical description, habitat, plant lore, is paralleled with 205 full-page photographs of flowering or fruiting plants. Nomenclature revised by Edward G. Voss. One of few works concerned with shrubs. 205 plates, 35 drawings. xxviii + 521pp. 21989-5 Paperbound $3.75

THE MUSHROOM HANDBOOK, Louis C. C. Krieger. Still the best popular handbook: full descriptions of 259 species, cross references to another 200. Extremely thorough text enables you to identify, know all about any mushroom you are likely to meet in eastern and central U. S. A.: habitat, luminescence, poisonous qualities, use, folklore, etc. 32 color plates show over 50 mushrooms, also 126 other illustrations. Finding keys. vii + 560pp. 21861-9 Paperbound $4.50

HANDBOOK OF BIRDS OF EASTERN NORTH AMERICA, Frank M. Chapman. Still much the best single-volume guide to the birds of Eastern and Central United States. Very full coverage of 675 species, with descriptions, life habits, distribution, similar data. All descriptions keyed to two-page color chart. With this single volume the average birdwatcher needs no other books. 1931 revised edition. 195 illustrations. xxxvi + 581pp. 21489-3 Paperbound $5.00

AMERICAN FOOD AND GAME FISHES, David S. Jordan and Barton W. Evermann. Definitive source of information, detailed and accurate enough to enable the sportsman and nature lover to identify conclusively some 1,000 species and sub-species of North American fish, sought for food or sport. Coverage of range, physiology, habits, life history, food value. Best methods of capture, interest to the angler, advice on bait, fly-fishing, etc. 338 drawings and photographs. 1 + 574pp. 6⅝ x 9⅜.
22196-2 Paperbound $5.00

THE FROG BOOK, Mary C. Dickerson. Complete with extensive finding keys, over 300 photographs, and an introduction to the general biology of frogs and toads, this is the classic non-technical study of Northeastern and Central species. 58 species; 290 photographs and 16 color plates. xvii + 253pp.
21973-9 Paperbound $4.00

THE MOTH BOOK: A GUIDE TO THE MOTHS OF NORTH AMERICA, William J. Holland. Classical study, eagerly sought after and used for the past 60 years. Clear identification manual to more than 2,000 different moths, largest manual in existence. General information about moths, capturing, mounting, classifying, etc., followed by species by species descriptions. 263 illustrations plus 48 color plates show almost every species, full size. 1968 edition, preface, nomenclature changes by A. E. Brower. xxiv + 479pp. of text. 6½ x 9¼.
21948-8 Paperbound $6.00

THE SEA-BEACH AT EBB-TIDE, Augusta Foote Arnold. Interested amateur can identify hundreds of marine plants and animals on coasts of North America; marine algae; seaweeds; squids; hermit crabs; horse shoe crabs; shrimps; corals; sea anemones; etc. Species descriptions cover: structure; food; reproductive cycle; size; shape; color; habitat; etc. Over 600 drawings. 85 plates. xii + 490pp.
21949-6 Paperbound $4.00

COMMON BIRD SONGS, Donald J. Borror. 33⅓ 12-inch record presents songs of 60 important birds of the eastern United States. A thorough, serious record which provides several examples for each bird, showing different types of song, individual variations, etc. Inestimable identification aid for birdwatcher. 32-page booklet gives text about birds and songs, with illustration for each bird.
21829-5 Record, book, album. Monaural. $3.50

FADS AND FALLACIES IN THE NAME OF SCIENCE, Martin Gardner. Fair, witty appraisal of cranks and quacks of science: Atlantis, Lemuria, hollow earth, flat earth, Velikovsky, orgone energy, Dianetics, flying saucers, Bridey Murphy, food fads, medical fads, perpetual motion, etc. Formerly "In the Name of Science." x + 363pp.
20394-8 Paperbound $3.00

HOAXES, Curtis D. MacDougall. Exhaustive, unbelievably rich account of great hoaxes: Locke's moon hoax, Shakespearean forgeries, sea serpents, Loch Ness monster, Cardiff giant, John Wilkes Booth's mummy, Disumbrationist school of art, dozens more; also journalism, psychology of hoaxing. 54 illustrations. xi + 338pp.
20465-0 Paperbound $3.50

THE PRINCIPLES OF PSYCHOLOGY, William James. The famous long course, complete and unabridged. Stream of thought, time perception, memory, experimental methods—these are only some of the concerns of a work that was years ahead of its time and still valid, interesting, useful. 94 figures. Total of xviii + 1391pp.
20381-6, 20382-4 Two volumes, Paperbound $9.00

THE STRANGE STORY OF THE QUANTUM, Banesh Hoffmann. Non-mathematical but thorough explanation of work of Planck, Einstein, Bohr, Pauli, de Broglie, Schrödinger, Heisenberg, Dirac, Feynman, etc. No technical background needed. "Of books attempting such an account, this is the best," Henry Margenau, Yale. 40-page "Postscript 1959." xii + 285pp.
20518-5 Paperbound $3.00

THE RISE OF THE NEW PHYSICS, A. d'Abro. Most thorough explanation in print of central core of mathematical physics, both classical and modern; from Newton to Dirac and Heisenberg. Both history and exposition; philosophy of science, causality, explanations of higher mathematics, analytical mechanics, electromagnetism, thermodynamics, phase rule, special and general relativity, matrices. No higher mathematics needed to follow exposition, though treatment is elementary to intermediate in level. Recommended to serious student who wishes verbal understanding. 97 illustrations. xvii + 982pp.
20003-5, 20004-3 Two volumes, Paperbound $10.00

GREAT IDEAS OF OPERATIONS RESEARCH, Jagjit Singh. Easily followed non-technical explanation of mathematical tools, aims, results: statistics, linear programming, game theory, queueing theory, Monte Carlo simulation, etc. Uses only elementary mathematics. Many case studies, several analyzed in detail. Clarity, breadth make this excellent for specialist in another field who wishes background. 41 figures. x + 228pp.
21886-4 Paperbound $2.50

GREAT IDEAS OF MODERN MATHEMATICS: THEIR NATURE AND USE, Jagjit Singh. Internationally famous expositor, winner of Unesco's Kalinga Award for science popularization explains verbally such topics as differential equations, matrices, groups, sets, transformations, mathematical logic and other important modern mathematics, as well as use in physics, astrophysics, and similar fields. Superb exposition for layman, scientist in other areas. viii + 312pp.
20587-8 Paperbound $2.75

GREAT IDEAS IN INFORMATION THEORY, LANGUAGE AND CYBERNETICS, Jagjit Singh. The analog and digital computers, how they work, how they are like and unlike the human brain, the men who developed them, their future applications, computer terminology. An essential book for today, even for readers with little math. Some mathematical demonstrations included for more advanced readers. 118 figures. Tables. ix + 338pp.
21694-2 Paperbound $2.50

CHANCE, LUCK AND STATISTICS, Horace C. Levinson. Non-mathematical presentation of fundamentals of probability theory and science of statistics and their applications. Games of chance, betting odds, misuse of statistics, normal and skew distributions, birth rates, stock speculation, insurance. Enlarged edition. Formerly "The Science of Chance." xiii + 357pp.
21007-3 Paperbound $2.50

MATHEMATICAL PUZZLES FOR BEGINNERS AND ENTHUSIASTS, Geoffrey Mott-Smith. 189 puzzles from easy to difficult—involving arithmetic, logic, algebra, properties of digits, probability, etc.—for enjoyment and mental stimulus. Explanation of mathematical principles behind the puzzles. 135 illustrations. viii + 248pp.
20198-8 Paperbound $2.00

PAPER FOLDING FOR BEGINNERS, William D. Murray and Francis J. Rigney. Easiest book on the market, clearest instructions on making interesting, beautiful origami. Sail boats, cups, roosters, frogs that move legs, bonbon boxes, standing birds, etc. 40 projects; more than 275 diagrams and photographs. 94pp.
20713-7 Paperbound $1.00

TRICKS AND GAMES ON THE POOL TABLE, Fred Herrmann. 79 tricks and games— some solitaires, some for two or more players, some competitive games—to entertain you between formal games. Mystifying shots and throws, unusual caroms, tricks involving such props as cork, coins, a hat, etc. Formerly *Fun on the Pool Table*. 77 figures. 95pp.
21814-7 Paperbound $1.25

HAND SHADOWS TO BE THROWN UPON THE WALL: A SERIES OF NOVEL AND AMUSING FIGURES FORMED BY THE HAND, Henry Bursill. Delightful picturebook from great-grandfather's day shows how to make 18 different hand shadows: a bird that flies, duck that quacks, dog that wags his tail, camel, goose, deer, boy, turtle, etc. Only book of its sort. vi + 33pp. 6½ x 9¼. 21779-5 Paperbound $1.00

WHITTLING AND WOODCARVING, E. J. Tangerman. 18th printing of best book on market. "If you can cut a potato you can carve" toys and puzzles, chains, chessmen, caricatures, masks, frames, woodcut blocks, surface patterns, much more. Information on tools, woods, techniques. Also goes into serious wood sculpture from Middle Ages to present, East and West. 464 photos, figures. x + 293pp.
20965-2 Paperbound $2.50

HISTORY OF PHILOSOPHY, Julián Marías. Possibly the clearest, most easily followed, best planned, most useful one-volume history of philosophy on the market; neither skimpy nor overfull. Full details on system of every major philosopher and dozens of less important thinkers from pre-Socratics up to Existentialism and later. Strong on many European figures usually omitted. Has gone through dozens of editions in Europe. 1966 edition, translated by Stanley Appelbaum and Clarence Strowbridge. xviii + 505pp.
21739-6 Paperbound $3.50

YOGA: A SCIENTIFIC EVALUATION, Kovoor T. Behanan. Scientific but non-technical study of physiological results of yoga exercises; done under auspices of Yale U. Relations to Indian thought, to psychoanalysis, etc. 16 photos. xxiii + 270pp.
20505-3 Paperbound $2.50

Prices subject to change without notice.
Available at your book dealer or write for free catalogue to Dept. GI, Dover Publications, Inc., 180 Varick St., N. Y., N. Y. 10014. Dover publishes more than 150 books each year on science, elementary and advanced mathematics, biology, music, art, literary history, social sciences and other areas.